The Dark l

A Dutiful Son

Pascal Bruckner

A Dutiful Son

Translated by Mike Mitchell

Dedalus

Dedalus would like to thank the French Ministry of Culture in Paris for its assistance in producing this book and Arts Council, England for its support of the Dedalus publishing programme.

Published in the UK by Dedalus Limited
24-26, St Judith's Lane, Sawtry, Cambs, PE28 5XE
email: info@dedalusbooks.com
www.dedalusbooks.com

ISBN printed book 978 1 910213 16 2
ISBN ebook 978 1 910 213 17 9

Dedalus is distributed in the USA by SCB Distributors
15608 South New Century Drive, Gardena, CA 90248
email: info@scbdistributors.com web: www.scbdistributors.com

Dedalus is distributed in Australia by Peribo Pty Ltd.
58, Beaumont Road, Mount Kuring-gai, N.S.W. 2080
email: info@peribo.com.au

First published by Dedalus in 2015

Printed in Finland by Bookwell
Typeset by Marie Lane

The Author

Pascal Bruckner was born 15 December 1948 in Paris. He is one of the "New Philosophers" who came to prominence in the 1970s and 1980s. Much of his work has been devoted to critiques of French society and culture.

His fiction includes *Lunes de fiel* which was made into the film *Bitter Moon* by Roman Polanski and *My Little Husband* published by Dedalus in 2013. His essays and novels have been translated into more than thirty languages and received worldwide acclaim.

The Translator

Mike Mitchell has translated more than seventy books from German and French.

His translation of Rosendorfer's *Letters Back to Ancient China* won the 1998 Schlegel-Tieck Translation Prize after he had been shortlisted in previous years for his translations of *Stephanie* by Herbert Rosendorfer and *The Golem* by Gustav Meyrink. His translations have been shortlisted four times for The Oxford Weidenfeld Translation Prize: *Simplicissimus* by Johann Grimmelshausen in 1999, *The Other Side* by Alfred Kubin in 2000, *The Bells of Bruges* by Georges Rodenbach in 2008 and the *Lairds of Cromarty* by Jean Pierre Ohl in 2013.

His recent translations from French include *Where Tigers are at Home* by Jean-Marie Blas de Roblès, *My Little Husband* by Pascal Bruckner and *Ink in the Blood* by Stéphanie Hochet.

Ingmar Bergman: The creative juices flow when the soul is threatened.

Saying my Prayers

It's bedtime. Kneeling at the foot of my bed, head bowed, hands together, I murmur my prayer in a low voice. I'm ten. After a brief review of the day's sins, I make a request of God, our all-powerful Creator. He knows how regularly I attend mass, how fervently I receive communion, how I love Him above all else. I simply ask Him, implore Him, to bring about the death of my father, while driving if possible. Brakes failing while he's going downhill, black ice, a plane tree, whatever suits Him best.

'I leave the choice of accident to you, God, see to it that my father kills himself.'

My mother arrives to tuck me in and read me a story. She looks at me tenderly. I intensify my fervour, put on an air of devotion. I close my eyes and say under my breath, 'I'm leaving you now, God, Maman's just come into my bedroom.'

She's proud of my ardent faith and at the same time worried that one day I might be tempted to become a priest. I get up at six in the morning to go and serve at mass in the Jesuit Collège Saint-Joseph, the junior secondary school I attend in Lyons, and I've already brought up the possibility of going to the *Petit Séminaire* for my baccalauréat years. It's a low mass, a short one, that is, I'm not qualified for the long ceremonies requiring a complex liturgy. When I get lost, I cross myself, it gives me composure. At that early hour there aren't many people in the church, not much more than a sparse scattering of devout old women straight out of bed muttering their prayers. I'm God's little eager beaver: the smell of the incense intoxicates me just as the priest intoxicates himself, filling his cruets with cheap white plonk and knocking back a full one himself as early as seven in the morning. His glazed expression makes us giggle. Lighting the candles sends me into raptures, I love this moment of contemplation before lessons. I receive communion, I adore the taste of the host, that unleavened bread that melts on your tongue like a biscuit. It fills me with strength, I mumble my Latin responses without understanding them, which makes them all the more beautiful. I serve at mass with sycophantic ardour – I want to have the best marks in paradise. When I screw up my eyes, it seems to me that Jesus is sending an affectionate wink in my direction.

Two years later, on the occasion of my solemn communion, I indulge in an orgy of goodness. I smile at everyone, the Angel of Good himself is living inside me. With sensual pleasure I sniff my new gilt-edged missal, the pages of which rustle when you turn them. I'm floating above the ground in my alb, I'm bathing in unction. Uncles and aunts cover me in kisses that I in turn freely lavish on my cousins. My zeal fills my mother with pride and a secret concern. It is good to have faith but within limits: the town of Lyons, former centre of the silk industry, is full of wretched abbés in stained cassocks and worn-out boots, the whipping boys of their hierarchy, the laughing stock of the street urchins, the proletarians of the Roman Catholic Apostolic Church. Many of them die young, abused and exhausted.

'Hurry up and get into bed, it's late already.'

'Yes, Maman, right away. Just one more minute, I haven't finished yet.'

I quickly go over the sins I've committed that day, adding two or three just as later on I will add a few items of income to my tax return in case I've omitted something more important. I thank the Lord for all His goodness towards me.

'Please, God, get rid of him, I'll be very good.'

My mother has no inkling of what's troubling her little cherub, all she sees in me is innocence and sweetness. The reason for my request to the Almighty goes back several weeks.

I have some geometry homework that I decide to finish after dinner. I skip it and go to bed, maths not being one of my strong points. My father comes to enlighten me and when I stubbornly persist in not understanding anything, he gets impatient. The more he tries to explain things to me, the less I understand. I'm tired. His advice is followed by shouts, his shouts by howls of rage accompanied by smacks. I'm an imbecile, a disgrace to the family. He's huge, so very imposing. A few minutes later I'm on the floor, I curl up in a ball to escape his blows, I slip under the bed from which his powerful hand drags me out in order to instil the rudiments of arithmetic in me. But above all, and this is what I cannot forgive myself, I beg him to spare me. 'Have mercy, Papa, have mercy, I'll work very hard. Please stop.'

The clouts, the kicks don't really matter. They hurt but the pain goes away. But to humiliate yourself before your torturer, to beg him to spare you because you've seen a murderous gleam in his eye, that's inexcusable.

Later on, when watching detective films, I will always

deplore the tendency of the victims to beg their killers' mercy. It arouses their sadism instead of making them relent. If one has to die, it should be with dignity. My mother comes upstairs, separates us, gives me a long hug while I'm still sobbing, my cheeks bright red. Afterwards my father comes to give me a kiss.

'Right then, let's make peace. We'll finish everything off tomorrow morning.'

I mumble a faint 'yes' but resentment has taken hold of me. It's a pool of pus that gradually seeps into every one of my thoughts. War has been declared: there will be armistices, often happy ones, intervals of harmony, but something has started that will never stop. Even when we're playing in the evening, under the sheets, at being in a sleigh on an icefield surrounded by wolves, I don't go along with it any more. Now it's him who's the carnivore about to devour me. The blind trust I used to have in him has been broken.

God doesn't answer my prayers and four years later I stop believing in Him. Until then every evening, or almost, I hear the metal gate open and see the lights of his car on the drive. I go upstairs to shut myself in my room, disappointed and tense. My mother tidies her hair and goes out onto the doorstep to brave the storm. During the night I dream that my body has left my bed and is floating through the air. I'm stuck to the ceiling, as if I were paragliding. I want to stay hanging in the stratosphere, to see the world from above without having to share in its trials and tribulations.

Brutal fathers have one advantage: they don't lull you with their gentleness, their sentimentality, they don't try to play at being big brothers or mates. They wake you up like an electric shock, make you someone who's eternally fighting or eternally oppressed. What mine passed on to me was his fury and for that I'm grateful. The hatred he instilled in me also saved me. I sent it back at him like a boomerang.

Part One

Horrible and Marvellous Days

Chapter 1

His Majesty Koch's Bacillus

We'd set off during the night, a troop of little imps in bobble hats, holding each others' hands, led by the nurses. The air was an ice crystal, burning our throats and lungs. The flakes, falling in their thousands, were so hard they scourged our faces, hurt like crystals. The snow crunched under our soles, muffling our steps. The wind was tearing it off the roofs of the chalets, reducing it to powder in gusts, transforming the darkness into a maelstrom of white. Each one of us saw his comrades transformed into moving statues from which plumes of vapour rose with every breath. We sang Christmas carols, *O Tannenbaum, Stille Nacht,* to keep our spirits up.

The road was closed to traffic, apart from the horse-drawn sleighs, jingling as they carried families wrapped up warm in blankets. When we looked up we could just about make out the distorted range of the Vorarlberg peaks. Everything was urging us to hurry up. Everyone was afraid of leaving the troop, being forgotten, buried under the white shroud. Inevitably one of us, ground down by cold and fear, would have an accident and his underpants would have to be changed quickly and it would earn the poor lad the name *Buxenschiss* (someone who dirties his pants). Finally the stained-glass windows of the church appeared: we climbed the steps into the graveyard where the crowd of parishioners was already gathering for midnight mass. After the hostile outdoors there was the warm atmosphere of a mountain Christmas with hymns and organ. The building had nothing of the Tyrolean buildings with onion-shaped domes and extravagant decoration: it was an unpretentious church with ochre walls, a pencil-shaped, black-slate steeple and a very bare nave. Close by the altar was a fir tree decorated with balls of various colours, a stucco St Nicholas, silver *lametta* and wobbly candles from which the wax dripped down, threatening to set the tree on fire. Two buckets of water had been provided in case of accident. A blond angel was stuck at the top of the tree, its wings spread wide as a sign of mercy. A huge crib housed Jesus, Mary, Joseph and all the other figures, made of terracotta that were as tall as we were. We were waiting for the moment when the donkey and the bull were going to turn their heads and start to bray or moo. The congregation consisted of mountain folk, rough farmers or stockbreeders in leather trousers, women in floral skirts and traditional headdresses. The war had finished barely six years ago, the French occupation of Vorarlberg had ended between 1947 and 1948. The majority of the congregation were women: many of the men were perhaps still prisoners of war or dead.

Our attention was drawn to the *Dorftrottel*, the village idiot, a boy of about fifteen with a goitre, close-cropped hair and a simpleton's face, whose task it was to amuse the congregation while they were waiting for the service to begin. He mimed a farcical version of the mass, making his audience roar with laughter. He's the one we'll bombard with snowballs, sometimes stones, later on, when we leave, under the indulgent eye of the priest. Having made fun of the service, he'd earned this little punishment. The priest intervened when the clown was on the ground and started to cry. The village choir, accompanied by a small local orchestra, sang Mozart's *Coronation Mass* with magnificent incompetence. The soprano, a simple innkeeper from the village, went up so high her voice seemed to have reached breaking point, she threw the orchestra into a panic, but got her breath back and finished the aria, exhausted. In that little European church Mozart's music lifted up the souls of these boors who, not long ago, had been involved in the defence of the *Reich*. Even today I cannot hear the *Laudate Dominum* without getting a lump in my throat. Exhausted by the lateness of the hour, drowsy from the heat, I generally fell asleep at the *Agnus Dei* to wake up at the end of the mass, roused from my sleep by the bells ringing out and the prospect of presents. The congregation were drinking mulled wine spiced with cinnamon, wishing each other a Happy Christmas and lighting candles on their parents' graves in the cemetery. Many left on skis, long runners turned up at the end simply attached to their boots with straps.

It was the fifties in the Kleinwalsertal, a remote district of Vorarlberg, an Austrian enclave in Bavaria. Suffering from a primary infection from having played in the dirty blankets of an uncle with renal tuberculosis, the family disease par excellence, I had been sent to a *Kinderheim* (children's home) in Mittelberg, a little village at 1,200 metres above sea level, when I was one and a half. I gabbled a German dialect before French and my mother who, to her great disappointment, I called *Mutti*, had for several years been obliged to engage a bilingual governess, Frau Rhuff, as interpreter. The woman's brother, mentally ill, had been killed as part of the *Gnadentod* ('mercy killing' as Adolf Hitler called it) programme without her knowing precisely whether he'd been gassed in a hermetically sealed truck or finished off with a lethal injection. The Vorarlberg dialect, close to Bavarian, was a language of farmers, as hard as granite, of jealously self-enclosed mountain tribes. It sounded as if you were gargling gravel and made you force out the vowels, so harshly did the consonants hit the palate. My parents came from Paris to see me and my mother stayed on, alone with me for a few weeks longer. At that time the journey in a Renault 4CV took almost 24 hours, especially in winter when you were faced with snowstorms and icy roads.

On the evening of Christmas Day I went back with them to the hotel where they were staying, a little guest house called *Kaffee Anna*. The fir trees lined the route; with the piles of snow on their branches they looked like servants in livery carrying parcels. We got to their room in the inn: at the foot of another tree, a miniature one this time, magnificently decorated and bearing sweets and other delicacies, were the presents in their glittering wrapping, some hidden deep within the branches. Since then the fir has for me always been the tree in whose shade presents grow. Every year I was given a model railway carriage or an engine. When I was very young my father put together a magnificent *Märklin* electric train for me that he later set up at home, in France. He would spend hours up in the attic and after several years he had created an entire region with its town, its tram, its hills, its cable car, its pedestrians, its cars, two or three stations, tunnels and viaducts. Under the table was a skein of electric wires. Model railways and, more generally, his love of trains and the work of a railwayman was a passion he passed on to me. I never ceased to be delighted by the details, precise down to the last millimetre, and the variety of the models I was given – a chemical pellet dissolved in the chimney of the steam locomotives made smoke. To reconstruct the world on a small scale instead of mastering it, that is the potent pleasure of model-building. The world in miniature turns us into occasional gods endowed with absolute power. Enveloped in solicitude, I looked out of the windows marbled with ice. The blizzard intensified and the great forest, of which I held a richly bedecked hostage prisoner in my room, trembled, filling me with terror.

Since then going to the Alps has been to return to childhood, to the land of toys, funicular railways, bells hanging round the cows' necks, places that look like toy villages, openwork balconies, frescoes painted on the farmhouses. I love the old-fashioned civilities, the simple rites of alpine cultures, even the omnipresence of milk in the food. Every time I get somewhere above 1,000 metres, I'm at home, in my landscape of the mind. I'm even moved by the yodel, that joyful sobbing in the throat that went from Switzerland to country music with its trills, its quarter tones and the easy-going accompaniment of the accordion. It's the inhospitality of the mountains that attracts me: they welcome you with a rejection, forcing you to face vertiginous cliffs, the mineral hardness of the ridges, the deceptive stillness of the glaciers. And when I set off for the peaks, racked by a fear that delights me as much as it makes me feel queasy, it is in the hope of finding, on my return, my old friend the fir tree. For me its tongue will always be the prattle of early childhood. Wherever that commoner among trees grows, in the shade and the north wind, there is babbling, sudden bursts of laughter. It remains the tree of an impalpable frontier separating platitude from altitude, the sentinel that welcomes us to the realm of height. Reaching up to the sky, it awaits the snow, ready to assume the burden for which it so obviously seems destined. When the flakes finally arrive, it lets itself be covered, its branches be decked with a thick coating of white, and wakes in the morning glittering with icicles, capturing the light with its needles. All day long its extremities, studded with tiny jewels, crack and crumble.

To the emotions it arouses can be added another: being the tree of hearth and home. Rimbaud cursed winter because it was 'the season of comfort'. That is precisely what makes it dear to me. I love those little villages clustered round a church and a mountain stream with its refreshing murmur, those wooden chalets with low ceilings, clean and scented furniture, box beds covered with a thick white duvet awaiting the traveller. Every room radiates opulence and simplicity, every nook and cranny seems to be a snug little cubby hole. And for me the falling snow creates a sense of intimacy, it gathers people together, appeals to the bashful lover, the sedentary hermit inside us. Unlike the rain, that mindlessly follows the law of gravity, the snow falls nobly, just kisses the cornices, consents to settle on a cushion prepared by other flakes. It muffles the noises, hides the ugliness we spread around us, gives a feeling of immobility as if, after having agreed to fall, it were slowly rising up from the ground to the sky. It isn't cold, it warms your heart, becomes the subtle enhancer of desire. Whenever, in the mountains, I open my eyes on a night rendered blue by full, soft flakes, I imagine I can see standing out, enigmatic and kind-hearted, against the snow-hooded branches, the face of the woman I love running towards me.

I was born in Paris, right at the end of 1948, during the weeks when the last German prisoners of war were released from the French internment camps. It was also the year in which Dr Theodor Morell, the Führer's personal physician, died. He was a notorious charlatan who prescribed for him drugs to counter impotence, constipation, diarrhoea, insomnia, spasms, all in all 90 different substances that were as much responsible for Hitler's death as the defeat of the *Wehrmacht*. It was a miracle that I survived: declared dead at birth, I was blue when I emerged, my umbilical cord wound round my neck. It took an hour of immersion in water, cold and hot, to revive me. Coming out I had damaged my mother so badly that she could never have another child. Suffering from rickets, weak bone mineralisation, then consumption, as they called it at the time, I became, in compensation, a spoilt son. My parents, despite not being particularly well-off, heaped presents on me. In return, death and disease were my companions from the very start: everyone around me was identified by the ailment they suffered from – angina, poliomyelitis, cancer, arthritis – it was the price to be paid for belonging to humanity. A child doesn't understand the adult world but he can still see its strengths and weaknesses. My uncle, Louis Marc, the one who'd transmitted the Koch bacillus to me, was the condemned man of my mother's family. It was as if he'd been born with a red cross of the plague on his back: he died young, at thirty-seven, so that his brothers and sisters could survive him. My mother's hero wasn't just the priest, at that time still omnipresent in French society, but the doctor, the keeper of our fates who held our fragile organisms in his hands and decided with a single word who had the right to live or to pass on. According to my mother, I was frail and sickly, likely to die while young or to survive only if I took things easy.

I can still hear her saying to the elder sister of a girlfriend I was 'going out with', 'If my son makes love every day, it'll kill him.' (I was nineteen at the time.)

Our lives were ruled by the Grim Reaper, we were corpses living on borrowed time, compelled to keep ourselves snug and warm. That was the price of our existence. As my first name indicated, I would never be able to fly with my own wings, I was the paschal lamb of Christian tradition that is immolated at Easter and that has to be cosseted before the sacrifice.

Whilst waiting for death, I spent eight years in the mountains, first in Austria, then in Switzerland, in Leysin, at Mademoiselle Rivier's. Days of enchantment. I managed, by the magic of childhood, to transform adversity into happiness. The torment I felt, especially the separation from my mother, faded with the discovery of the beauty of the Alps and of being part of a group. If it doesn't do away with you, illness raises you up, turns you into the scion of an aristocracy. Your pathology becomes the equivalent of a title of nobility. Finding among some family papers a certificate from Immenstadt Hospital in the Allgäu prescribing massive injections of penicillin for me, fills me with rather puerile joy. I really had been ill and lived in that area, I was a child of *Mitteleuropa,*[1] I could lay claim to a tradition to which I could remain faithful, that was where my *Heimat* (my home) was. In taking me away from my parents, the disease was just as much a piece of good fortune as the antibiotics that cured me. Fifty years earlier I would have given up the ghost surrounded by others, coughing up streams of blood. That is the cruel side of modern illnesses: they kill off those who haven't been able to hold on until the miracle cure arrives. The progress of medicine has transformed death. I spent very happy days in preventoriums, sanatoriums, convalescent homes, with the smell of mustard poultices, sulphur fumigation and the burning suction of the cupping glasses that were heated over a flame. Far from my parents, I learnt about freedom very early on. In

1 Literally 'Central Europe' but the German term is laden with cultural and political connotations.

Leysin, the 'Davos of French-speaking Switzerland' – where, as I was to learn fifty years later, Michel Simon, Albert Camus and Roland Barthes had already spent time – the joyous commotion of the dormitories, my first loves, the whispering of the children, while outside roe deer and chamois were running through the snow with muffled steps, was absolute bliss. The treatment is a comforting ritual: obligatory siesta, in the sun if possible, wrapped in a blanket, temperature taken every afternoon, a barefoot run in the snow, recommended for its therapeutic effect, analysis of phlegm discharged, enemas, weekly check-ups and, for the worst affected, discreet removal to the nearby hospital. We were looked after by tall women, dedicated and austere, who seemed to have renounced any personal life. We were their adopted children. Later on I was to learn that many of the little patients were Jews. Ten years after the end of the war their identity continued to be concealed, they were called by assumed names, as if people were afraid the *Wehrmacht* ogre might reappear. And when I spoke German, they automatically replied in French in order to erase that cursed language from my memory. I remember crying while watching the film *Heidi*, the story of a young girl who's forced to leave her Alpine village to go and live in Bern with a relative. In a heart-rending scene she climbs to the top of a bell-tower in an attempt to see her home, between two mountains. But what a piece of luck, though it might not seem so, to escape from your family and find yourself independent at such a young age and in full possession of your powers!

Very early on I developed a taste for pranks, even ones of a dubious nature, a solid survival instinct, a narcissism that saved me from much hurt and, above all, a sense of merriment. I was the lad who made the girls laugh, running naked into their rooms just to hear their shrieks. Or I would slip into a bathroom with one of the girls to compare our anatomies. If we were caught, the punishment was mild. What was a slap or being shut up in the 'black corridor', a passage with no lights, compared to the mysteries revealed?

Tuberculosis was a family disease: all my uncles and aunts had caught it, one of my cousins, Marie Eugenie who was with me in Leysin, had contracted it after being bitten by a dog and two of my distant relatives had died of it, including my paternal grandmother who died at Hauteville-Lompnes in the department of Ain in 1936, sent on her way with the sarcastic remarks of her husband, who accused her of abandoning him. To all the letters she sent him – he was Belgian and lived in Antwerp – he replied by underscoring every one of her spelling mistakes with a thick line. Hauteville is a charmless little place in the foothills of the Jura, some fifty kilometres from Geneva. Situated at 900 metres above sea level, it is entirely devoted to physical disorders: sanatoriums, oncology and addiction centres nowadays, not forgetting the inevitable establishments for Alzheimer's and old people's homes. All the upper part of the village has been taken over by anonymous buildings populated by ghosts in wheelchairs or hobbling along on sticks. My father, then an adolescent, and his brother and sister, very disturbed at the loss of their mother and abandoned by their father, were taken in there by the Bavuz family, decent folk who made mattresses, chairs and sofas, wielding the large needles with great dexterity. Their two sons, nice boys though not terribly bright, members of the Ain *maquis* led by Henri Romans-Petit, succumbed to alcohol after the war. Eventually the elder, one day when he was plastered, picked a quarrel with his younger brother, started beating him up then finished him off by pumping him full of buckshot. He ended his days in the lunatic asylum.

When I was little I often used to go and spend my holidays with them: the air was good, the food was good, they were generous. I spent the whole day out in the field with other boys: we made slings for ourselves, daggers from sharpened bits of metal and killed all the animals that came within our reach out of a sort of automatic devilry. We put splinters of glass in molehills so that the creatures would cut open their snouts when they came up to breathe, nailed toads alive to barn walls, shot tits and swifts with catapults, hunted for adders, slow-worms and grass snakes that we cut up into slices, set cats' or dogs' tails on fire with lighter fuel.

There were three tests facing any stranger who wanted to join the gang: first you had to hold a wasp or a bee in your hand for a whole minute without showing any reaction to the stings; then to steal the litter of a cat that had just given birth and drown the kittens. I did it one morning: I knocked the kittens out on the stone wall of an open-air washing place before putting them in a jute sack that I held under water. I can still see the little bubbles, pink with blood, rising to the surface, and recall it with horror. The third test was to go to the village abattoir. Every time I went past the prefabricated building the cries of the pigs in their death throes made my blood run cold. That day a farmer had brought a calf that, sensing the approach of death, was resisting with all its might and bellowing its despair. Three men grasped it and, taking care to avoid its flailing hooves, hung it upside down by its two hind legs. The butcher, a fearsome figure to my eyes in his killer's uniform, done up in an apron with large knives and cleavers hanging over it, stunned it with a bludgeon blow on the back of its head, cut its throat with a broad-bladed knife and almost immediately, while the animal was still convulsing, cut off its tail and started to eviscerate it prior to removing its hide.

You had to watch the ceremony standing up, without batting an eyelid. Life in the country rarely teaches you to love nature, it is first and foremost a school of cruelty.

It was there that I also discovered the American science fiction comics that were forbidden at home: the invasion of giant spiders released by a nuclear war, the deadly woodlice and mice, the giant earthworms that came out of the shower heads and strangled humans, the toads that gobbled up men. I loved the *Pieds nickelés*, those anarchic idlers and swindlers, and *Pim, Pam, Poum,* the French version of the *The Katzenjammer Kids* (i.e. the 'hangover kids'), the comic strip by Rudolph Dirks first published in the *New York Journal* in 1897. It was inspired by Wilhelm Busch's stories in pictures of *Max und Moritz* that I had grown up with in my early years, together with *Struwwelpeter – Shock-headed Peter*, a book of illustrated sadistic rhymes about a little rebel who has his fingers chopped off as punishment for sucking his thumb or is drowned in his soup when he refuses to eat it. And of course there were the *Tintin* albums that literally brought me back into the world and that I reread every three years as well as the less well-known *Jo, Zette et Jocko*, the brother and sister with their monkey. It was Hergé who first gave me a taste for Asia, above all for India, when I read the adventures of Tintin and Snowy when they were staying at the palace of the Rajah of Gaipajama in *The Pharaoh's Cigars* and *The Blue Lotus.*

The Katzenjammer Kids are two rascals who live with their family on the tropical island of Bongo that is ruled over by an idle king. They never cease to make life a misery for two bearded adults, the Captain and the Astronomer, stealing cakes made by their aunt, always making others take the blame. When they're caught red-handed they're given a good hiding with a rolling pin that leaves them laid up for weeks. Later on I drew inspiration from this edifying reading to play all sorts of dirty tricks on my nearest and dearest: a banana skin slipped under their feet, whoopee cushions, buckets of water balanced on half-open doors (my mother was almost knocked out by one), liquids poured into shoes, plastic turds, dead mice slipped between the sheets, apple-pie beds, rabbit droppings scattered in the soup.

Memory is a strange sieve. In my childhood horrendous and fantastic things went cheek by jowl and for a long time I only retained what was good about it. You have to forget in order to survive, clear out the memories that prevent you from making progress. I very quickly created an inviolable refuge, a sort of psychological fortress where I could escape from the cries, the physical abuse of the grown-ups. As an only child the very nature of things meant that from the start I was not so much loved as put first. Unsuited for trials and tribulations, blessed with the ability to find pleasure in disagreeable situations, I was my mother's darling boy and her only wish was to anticipate and satisfy the least of my desires. This fostered as much as distorted my development: it left me with the sense of being a winner, the assurance that there was a place for me here on earth, the confidence that I had been born under a lucky star even if, during adolescence, my upbringing was to undergo a brutal change. I had to be kept at home by hook or by crook, kept away from the world and its corrupting influences. Tuberculosis, the wound that could have killed me, gave me a taste for life. Illness teaches us nothing if not that it can be overcome; in that sense it, too, saved me.

But at the time when I arrived in that desolate hamlet in the Kleinwalsertal, eaten away by Koch's bacillus, I was far from suspecting that my father had hidden there for six whole months, in the spring of 1945, with his Austrian mistress, in order to escape from the Soviet troops and avoid the Allied authorities. He was to send me back there six years later, taking advantage of my infection to turn me into a good little German-speaker.

Chapter 2

Conjugal Endearments

It's lunchtime. I'm going to the kitchen to take the dishes into the dining room, I must be twelve. I hear the first howls of fury, like a series of detonations, a well-known tune. We're living on the outskirts of Lyons, in a house with a big garden beside the N7. Across the road the countryside begins, cows and sheep are grazing in the meadows on the other side of the wall, giving off a strong animal smell. In the distance you can see the turrets of a castle, the heights of Ecully. Below is a railway line that's only used by goods trains. The shouts get louder, my mother calls for help. I dash in, it's almost a ritual but this time it seems more serious. My father's calling my mother a stupid woman, she replies with dirty swine, he's knocking her about with violent slaps to the head, she's trying to pull his hair. They're both of them scarlet with rage. She's struggling, grabs him. It's a clumsy brawl, the only thing that counts is the sound level of the combatants.

'You're seeing your tart again, you bastard!' she yells.

He confirms that. 'Yes, you crazy bitch, I've gone back to her. Have you had a look at yourself, the way you are, you apology of a woman? I'll have you put away!'

He's trying to smash her head against the wall.

'Stop it, stop it,' I beg them.

The entangled pair sway and almost fall over, as if in an interrupted waltz. In the course of the confrontation my father jams my mother's hand in the partly open door, he's going to crush her fingers. I put my body in the way, at the last moment I manage to push the door back. She, panting with rage, hadn't even seen the danger; he's wondering whether to give her one more clout or to wallop me to teach me not to get involved in things that are no business of mine. He lets go, grabs his car keys and goes out, slamming the door behind him.

My mother's crying, crimson-faced. She apologises, 'Aren't we stupid, eh? Making an exhibition of ourselves like that. Come and have your lunch, quick, it's getting cold.'

But the tablecloth has been pulled off, the plates are on the floor, broken, the dining room's a battlefield, the soup's a green waterfall dripping onto the floor. I'm not hungry any more, I think I burst into tears as well. We pick up the debris, the pieces of glass, and mop up the soup.

I was trying to defend my mother but did I defend her enough?

Twenty years later, in the early eighties, despite the fact that I'm grown up, I sometimes go back for Sunday lunch with my parents, who now live in Paris, Porte d'Auteuil. It's the force of tradition. And exactly the same scenario is played out. The meal starts fairly normally until, on some pretext or other – too much salt in the salad, a bitter radish, a dropped spoon – the first salvoes are fired.

My mother goes pale, asks my father to desist. 'Stop it, no one's interested in you.'

He goes on, so then, almost automatically, she starts coughing gently. That's fatal.

'What is that noise? Go and spit it out if you're ill.'

'I'm not ill, I'm just clearing my throat.'

The scene is set, I know the drama that's going to be played out off by heart. The tension rises imperceptibly until it reaches fever pitch. A minor incident is to escalate into a storm, the clouds are gathering. All the troubles, all the humiliations of the week are going to reach bursting point in the regular Sunday scene. My father needs to explode. Like an actor who's got into his stride, he goes off at a tangent, makes it look as if he's changing the subject. He starts up an anodyne conversation with me, a ruse to prepare his counter-attack. The about-turn comes suddenly. Mount Testy is rumbling, the eruption is imminent. He gives my mother a hard look.

'At least you could have dressed properly when your son's come to visit. Have you seen yourself in that get-up?' (His favourite expression.)

'Oh, leave me in peace…' Her words are accompanied by various glottal sounds.

'Are you at it again?'

'I've a frog in my throat, leave me alone.'

But the frog turns into a horned toad, suddenly my mother is convulsed with a hacking cough that forces her to get up. She's spluttering, going brick-red. Now my father has his pretext and war is declared.

'Will you stop it!'

He raises his right hand.

She's incapable of replying, racked by an irrepressible fit of coughing.

'If you don't stop, I'm leaving.'

'Well off you go, then.'

'Certainly not, you cretin. Now that's enough. If there's anyone who should leave, it's you.'

'No it's not,' she tries to say between two hiccoughs. 'I'm having lunch with my son. Don't start spoiling everything with your coarseness.'

Hardly has she finished that her neck swells up again, her cheeks bulge, a series of convulsions come to the surface from deep within her lungs. She's suffocating, writhing. My mother suffered from this hysterical cough all her life. As if she were giving her husband the chance to reprimand her. He used to forbid her to smoke; she smoked Craven A that came in elegant red tins with gold lettering that smelt of spicy tobacco. For her a modern woman owed it to herself to have a cigarette between her fingers. She was of medium height with some distant Spanish ancestry, black hair, merry eyes, a snub nose, wavy hair brushed up high over her forehead, as was the fashion in the post-war years. He corresponded to the stereotype Aryan as portrayed in propaganda: tall by the standards of the time, thick blond, almost ginger hair, grey-blue eyes, straight nose, broad forehead.

Once, in the 1960s, he'd thrown her out of a recital in Lyons given by the pianist Wilhelm Kempff because she'd twice shown a slight irritation of the mucous membrane. In that place the slightest murmur sounded like thunder. The maestro himself had shown signs of impatience, his beautiful virtuoso's hands, those two finely muscled thoroughbred animals that right through the war had played for the upper ranks of the National Socialist Party, had remained poised over the keyboard. The audience had expressed its disapproval by turning en bloc to face our row. My mother, banished from the concert, had had to wander round the corridors, her little explosions of sound swallowed up in the immense space. When I went to look for her, she'd already set off for the Place Bellecour Bus Station in order to make her way home. She got there long after us and, having missed out on Beethoven and Schubert, arrived back to be greeted, not surprisingly, by a whole recital of insults.

On this particular Sunday, in Paris twenty years later, my mother is trying to suppress the eructations coming from deep within her chest. I pat her on the back to help her get over it. Her lungs are whistling. My father roughly shoves me out of the way, grabs hold of her, starts to shake her.

'Will you stop it, for Christ's sake!'

The vicious circle has been set in motion. I push him aside but the lunch is spoilt. He gets up and goes off. It's another of his sham exits, he comes back, a nasty expression on his face. He's looking for her, he wants her, she's aroused the monster's bad temper and he's not going to let her get away. As if to give him another good reason, she explodes in a shower of phlegm and spittle, setting off a volley of roars opposite. The crescendo is well timed, the great organ starts to thunder. He threatens to overturn the table, to throw the food in her face. I stop him but he still manages to catch her full in the face with a glass of water 'to calm her down'. She's suffocating, trembling, her husband goes off to shut himself away in his study. At once the cough stops, my mother's shivering. In a soft voice, as if nothing had happened, she says, 'All the same, it is stupid when I cough like that. I'm sorry, Pascal dear.'

It's an automatic reaction I'm familiar with: victims accusing themselves of the persecution they suffer. I beg her to separate from him and she replies, 'You're right, you're right,' just to get me to leave her in peace. An hour later I go, my nerves in tatters. I feel soiled. I don't go back for six months. On the *métro* I meet my girlfriend of the time, a pretty woman, part West Indian, part Mexican, and burst into tears in her arms like a little boy. Today I wonder: shouldn't I have thumped my father as he deserved, given him a good hiding he wouldn't forget?

However, a distinction has to be made between these little changes of mood and the Great Storms of Abuse that, for preference, had to take place before witnesses, on the occasion of a dinner party. Then my father would really go to town, seeing the presence of outsiders, children or adults, as the perfect setting for his outbursts. The stage director prepared his effects. He would rub his hands, enjoying himself in anticipation: he had his victim and his audience, the show could begin. He would start the meal all smiles, put on a cheerful air. Which made the abrupt change all the more brutal. Had my mother had the misfortune to clink one of the glasses too hard or to knock one of the table legs? A fatal mistake! He would tell her off. 'Can't you be more careful?' She would apologise and immediately do the same again, which brought her a further reprimand – 'What a clumsy cow you are!' – that induced another blunder. Then he would move on from 'clumsy cow' to 'stupid bitch', marking the start of Act II. In a second the affable host was transformed into a raging lunatic: he raised his arms up to heaven and let them fall back heavily onto the table, making all the dishes tremble. If a nephew or cousin started to cry, he would go over the top, threatening them with the most terrible punishment. My mother would try to deflect these blows, offering herself up as a scapegoat. She would beg his pardon a thousand times over – too late. He would finally stand up, not without knocking over a few dishes, leaving the company exhausted, like some domestic Attila. Plates and glasses were only invented to allow irascible husbands to calm their nerves: the exasperating jingle-jangle they produce as they break is very soothing to the mind. Later on I was to use this kind of bolt-from-the-blue scenario in some of my novels. I have come across this trait in a few of my friends, men in an unhappy marriage who take pleasure in publicly belittling their wives, in their eyes the symbol of their failure in life. All those present come out of it feeling defiled.

They spent a day in Lyons in 1999, just six months before she died. My mother, very much weakened because of an encephalopathy that disturbed her motor functions, stumbled on the pavement and collapsed. Instead of helping her to get up, he called her an 'imbecile' in front of the astounded passers-by, told her she was just doing it to attract attention and left her lying there. It took three people to help her back onto her feet. He'd already cleared off and on the train back to Paris he called her all the names under the sun. One October evening a few weeks later she fell down outside a hotel in the Boulevard Saint-Jacques, where she had gone to buy the evening paper, and broke her thigh. She was seventy-nine. I dashed off to A & E at Cochin Hospital. My father swept into the room and, to the amazement of the nurse, bawled, 'I've had just about enough of your play-acting, you stupid moron. Get up and come home.'

I threw him out and forbade him to come back. During fifty years of marriage he was remarkably consistent in persecuting her and she was remarkably persevering in her submission. The systematic demolition of his wife took him hardly a year after their wedding, at the end of which my mother had her first epileptic fit. As she lay there in her bed she, who was an exemplary case of the acceptance of servitude, had looked at him, eyes wide, with a kind of amused astonishment. He stamped his feet. Her mind already elsewhere, she asked him in a faraway voice, 'What's happened, René dear, you look upset?'

She was about to play the worst trick imaginable on him, she was going to decline into dementia, die in a few months and deprive him of his favourite punch-bag. I am astounded that she went along with her torturer for such a long time, consented to that wretched living hell.

She hoped he would change, was banking on an improvement in his character. She would emphasise his good sides, which he did have of course, and quite a lot at that. She would seek out any argument that would justify her position as an abused wife. Day after day he would go on at her, persuading her that she was inferior, she was ugly. Arguments were the norm, peace the exception. At each insult she would bow her head, gradually conforming more and more to the mirror he held up to her, growing thinner, paler. What was worse, for twenty years she worked as his secretary, taking down his letters in shorthand without being paid. Dictation invariably degenerated as the loudmouth-in-chief added complaints connected with work to his usual grievances. The most charming epithets – slut, idiot, cretin – buzzed round the room like a swarm of wasps. She pretended not to feel the stings, concentrating on typing out his business correspondence on an old Remington. At the least mistake he would tear up the letter, forcing her to start all over again with a carbon copy. From my room I could hear him bellowing and would stick my fingers in my ears. Sometimes in the morning she would come to breakfast with swollen lips, traces of bruising on her arms that she tried to hide. When I pointed them out, she would say,

'I bumped into something, I'm very clumsy.'

She seemed to have been immunised against humiliation and tended to make a mountain out of a molehill, as the saying goes. Even at the best of times we lived under the threat of an imminent storm. It could break in the middle of the night, I would hear muttering on the other side of the wall followed by furious whispering, heavy objects falling with a crash, doors being slammed. Such outbursts are a very effective counter to the banality of everyday life, but when they're a daily occurrence, they become part of a routine. Afterwards he would beg her forgiveness by showering her with presents. She threw them back in his face.

Returning to the bosom of my family was like lifting a stone crawling with scorpions underneath. At one point my mother, having risen to the provincial middle classes now that the family's financial situation had improved since the early lean years, had the idea of organising bridge evenings with a few women friends. For the first three or four times these passed off fairly normally – until the day when the Despot, annoyed at this show of independence, burst into the room in the middle of a game and, on the pretext of an important report to be typed, flew into a terrible rage. The ladies scattered like frightened birds, my mother apologising profusely. She tried to invite them again but the shadow of the Tyrant hung over the house and bridge was relegated to the list of impossible pastimes. Thus it was that he created a void around her. After ten years of marriage she'd managed to gain her driving licence. One day he let her take the wheel, he himself sitting in the passenger seat guiding her; after driving for several kilometres she managed, in a nice subconsciously deliberate mistake, to drive the vehicle into the wall by the gate. Apart from the immediate slap she received, she was condemned to the moped for life, come rain or wind. She didn't dare ever to drive again.

All that didn't mean there weren't long periods of shared pleasures, discoveries, journeys. My father was very successful in his work. A mining engineer, he'd taken me with him underground several times: putting on his helmet and goggles he became a creature from hell. I believe his work involved measuring the levels of firedamp, checking the supports of the galleries, the fracturing of the rocks, the installation of the rails, the running of the trucks. (Much later on I was to learn that the German philosopher Friedrich Leibniz, himself an engineer in the Harz Silver Mines, had between 1680 and 1686 invented a system for draining water that was revolutionary in its time.) I was terrified by the vibrations of the lift, the loud voices of miners working stripped to the waist, the suffocating heat, the fearful darkness. The mine shafts seemed to me like pits into which disobedient children were thrown to let them rot away in the subterranean caverns. A former employee of the *Mines de la Sarre* and *Charbonnages de France*, my father was devastated to see the Alès, Forbach, Decazeville and Sarreguemines mines closed down. He was perhaps not wrong in that. Be that as it may, the fact remains that when he reached thirty, he began to enjoy the first rewards of his work. He'd started with a green Renault 4CV, that looked like a frog on wheels, moved on to a Panhard, then a Renault Frégate in the 60s before finally going over to the competition and ending up with a Citroën DS 19. We used to play with the automatic suspension that made the car go up and down. His aim was to gain the esteem of those around him, catch up with his brothers-in-law, who were more successful than him and with whom his wife, in a minor but legitimate act of vengeance, used to taunt him, calling him a failure whenever they quarrelled.

Each was the other's jailor. He was very proud of the fact that he had managed to escape from the working-class condition, to which his father's bankruptcy could have condemned him and which was that of his brother and sister. We were en route for the middle classes, the future looked rosy. The furniture changed, labour-saving appliances appeared in the house, sophisticated devices moved us to admiration or to laughter. We entertained. My parents' friends reminded me of Jolyon Wagg, the insurance agent and garrulous sponger who, with his innumerable offspring in tow, invades Marlinspike Hall in *Tintin*. What I did not see at the time was the racy blonde, very 1950s, showing a lot of cleavage, billing and cooing with her husband while she was already my father's mistress. We went on holiday to Spain and Portugal to visit our backward cousins bowed low under the rule of dictators my father had nothing against. He prided himself on his knowledge of modern art, bought daubs by Bernard Buffet and lithographs by Vasarley, for him the acme of the avant-garde. He was promoted, put on weight. He was cultured, showed impressive erudition in geography and science, made cupboards and chairs with his own hands, read the classics, was an excellent cook. For occasional visitors he presented an amiable, articulate façade. He used to hum popular airs: Charlus' 1903 '*Viens Poupoule*! *viens*!/*Quand j'entends des chansons*/*Ça me rend tout polisson*', Tino Rossi's '*Marinella*', Mistinguett's '*On dit que j'ai de belles gambettes*', Georges Brassens' '*Le Gorille*' or '*La Paloma*'.[2] My mother would frown, tell him to shut up, in order to keep such smutty popular ditties from my ears,

2 Charlus: 'Come on, Baby, come on!/When I hear these little songs/They really turn me on'; Mistinguett: 'They say I've got a lovely pair of legs'; in the Brassens song women eye a gorilla's private parts when it's in its cage, but flee when it escapes, determined to have sex somehow.

knowing that each of those tunes was associated with an affair.

But under the mask of social pride any discord could send him hurtling into a rage, the enjoyment of destruction. Being unable to gain our understanding, he would batter our eardrums remorselessly. Every person gives off a certain atmosphere, a general mood that is their wavelength. It follows them step by step, whatever they do, and etches itself on our memory as the synthesis of their passing. The tone of his was so dark that eventually it ate away at all our pleasures. He took a particularly malign pleasure in subjecting us to a series of difficult questions that brought out our ignorance and, by contrast, presented him as the fount of all knowledge. Every day we had a German test; we had to translate the most difficult expressions into the language of Goethe. We were stumped and if my mother did attempt an answer, she would get a dressing-down for her accent that my father would parody for the rest of the day by pursing his lips when he spoke. She and I were two children bowed under the tutelage of an omnipotent master. She was afraid of him, she kept saying, 'You father's so strong, he has so much energy.'

'No, he isn't, Maman; it's only your weakness that makes him strong.'

I, too, went in fear of him, I toed the line. When he terrorised me, bellowed at me, I swore I'd have my revenge. But, like all children, I also wanted to please him, gain his esteem, surprise him, make him laugh with the faces I pulled, the delightful remarks I made. I dreamt of him showering me with words of praise rather than caustic comments. I was upset when he told me off. But when he asked me the stupid question, 'Who do you like best, your Papa or your Maman?' (like all autocrats, he wanted to be loved) I couldn't find it in my heart to lie and invariably answered, 'Maman.' As a consequence of this domestic triangle our daily life was a system of alternating alliances: my father and my mother against me, my father and me against my mother, my mother and me against him, all of us against everyone else. And then one day it was me with the others and without them.

So, lacking our independence, she and I would go for strolls in the surrounding countryside. To be free is to be able to want and to do what you like. We were impotent. We would go alongside the railway track as far as the village of Charbonnières, past anonymous villas guarded by ferocious dogs. My mother went for walks instead of leaving for good. She fled all the better to return, chained to her torturer, who bullied her while having passionate affairs elsewhere. We trotted along all the better to submit once more to the whims of the Sovereign. She read the newspapers, feeding on the vicarious life of the nations, of other people, in order to forget her own. At every crisis she would exclaim, 'Oh là là, things are in a bad way…' and the banner headlines allayed her own misfortunes. Knowing that people elsewhere had to endure famine, massacres, floods, made her personal suffering less hard to bear. At home I learnt two contradictory things: passivity and hatred, the one fuelling the other.

Unable to live a life of her own, my mother very quickly started developing illnesses. One year after I was born she had her first epileptic fits, that continued until the end and terrified me. She took Gardenal, a phenobarbital, then Dekapine, recommended for the treatment of seizures. After a multitude of minor ailments and operations, she managed to poison herself with bismuth, that she took for ordinary intestinal contractions, and fell into a deep coma for several months, from which she recovered surrounded, for a while, with an aura of mystery and respect. After which – by this time I was already forty – she developed an encephalopathy and Parkinson's disease. She fell ill to get my father to attend to her, collected ailments to finally make herself visible, the way other people collect exotic countries. But these endless complaints alienated him even more. Her ravaged body exasperated him all the more as she went from one ailment to the next, like a nomad. The periods of health were nothing other than short bridges between between two relapses. She was a medical encyclopaedia in herself; it was a point of honour with her to catch bizarre variants, she got the most incongruous bacilli or viruses that left the doctors baffled. To the question, 'What have you done in your life?' she could have answered, 'Acquired a certain number of illnesses that I wear like so many decorations.' She wanted an honourable death on the battlefield of health. Schopenhauer compares human relations to those of porcupines. When they want to get warm, they huddle up together but injure themselves on their spines. So they withdraw, but then they get cold. They have to repeat this manoeuvre until they find the right distance and the pain inflicted by the spines becomes bearable. My mother had lost all her spines or, rather, had turned them in on herself.

Like her brothers and sisters, I begged her to get a divorce.

'That's not done in our family, you know. Divorced women have a very bad reputation.'

The youngest of a Catholic family of nine children, brought up in the sanctimony and disdain for the body at the Notre Dame de Sion School, where she was a boarder, she couldn't bring herself to contravene their rules in this way. Especially as she couldn't afford to live without the money from her husband. The financial argument was an excuse: when, later on, she obtained a position in the Finance Ministry and achieved a certain degree of economic independence, she stayed with him, this time on the pretext that he was mired in debt. The one who looked after the household, she ended up in old age depriving herself of everything while my father was simply throwing money around. She ate up the left overs, cheese rinds, hunks of stale bread, cut down on light, even on matches, grew visibly thinner, denied herself the least pleasure. At the end she was nothing more than skin and bone. Miserliness is a symptom of a disturbed mind: the impression she made on the outside world was that of a woman who was stinting herself. It was terrible to see her poorly dressed, uncaring of her appearance, losing her hair, walking with uncertain, trembling steps.

She was defeatism with a smile on its face. I often found her sad, her eyes moist from having cried, old before her time, not really understanding what was happening to her. To be able to sympathise with other people's suffering you need to grow, to stand at a distance from yourself. The winter days were long – I was at school, my father absent. She was bored, she would torment herself: where was he, what was he doing, with which 'tart' was he being unfaithful? Jealousy was a substitute for a life of her own. She even preferred him to hit her, at least it meant he was there. All women were her enemy and she hated the woman in herself. At Notre Dame de Sion the girls were only allowed to take a bath in their nightdresses. The need for hygiene counted less than the fear of nakedness: each pupil had a sense of disgust at her anatomy inculcated in her by the nuns. Her vocabulary for the female sex varied between 'silly goose', 'slut' and 'old bag'. They all wanted to 'hook' themselves a man: this term, derived from angling, summarised for her the relations between the sexes: bachelors were surrounded by scheming hussies or vamps determined to 'land' them. She had killed off all her femininity; she punished herself in order to punish my father. She used to rummage through his things, kept a list of his mistresses, sometimes rang them up to try and put them off. She gave me the letters and postcards he wrote to them to look after, setting up a dossier just in case. He engaged in epistolary adultery without taking any precautions, wanting to give his infidelities a literary veneer. I kept some of these missives: lyrical effusions and chit-chat. Nothing worth making a fuss about. It's the only thing I've forgiven him.

Later on my mother was to apply this misogyny to my first love affairs. If only she'd been able to sew up my penis or unscrew it and lock it up in a box! The female students I went around with were the devil incarnate, lascivious deceivers who were going to drain me of my substance. Whenever she came to see me, she would purloin some dirty clothes, especially items of underwear. She felt sick at the very idea of my taking these treasures to the laundrette and entrusting them to the anonymous rotations of a machine. She wanted to keep control of my body fluids, check for potential diseases, ensure that I wasn't abusing my youthful ardour. She was happy to travel right across Paris with two vests and a pair of underpants. Sometimes we would exchange these highly compromising goods under the table in a café. She sewed a little label with my name on all items, including my handkerchiefs. Every year we took part in the hunt for the missing sock: some single socks gave rise to investigations lasting several months during which my mother was transformed into Sherlock Holmes as she tried to recover the missing item. My father would join in. Their theories varied from negligence to organised theft – either I couldn't give a damn or a particularly crafty gang working for a group of one-legged men had specialised in stealing one sock at a time. I recall one amusing scene when, as I was coming out into the street after lunch with her, she called me from the window and shouted at the top of her voice, 'Pascal, your underpants, I've mended them. Catch.'

'My what?'

'Your blue underpants, you know, the ones you like best.'

Passers-by gathered and started to chant, 'Pascal, your underpants.'

I could have killed her and ordered her to shut up. Eventually we decided to have a good laugh about it. I loved her laugh, even her fits of giggles that brought the tears to her eyes. She once more became the young girl I'd never known, full of hopes and plans for the future. She'd gone to Brazil as a French teacher for two years when she was twenty, before coming back to Paris in 1940, at the declaration of hostilities, then entombing herself in the conjugal shroud.

At the age of thirty-seven, suffocating in a country I considered too cramped – to be French is an act of faith and I'd become an agnostic – I went to teach in California. My appointment was a matter of pure luck. Having had two books translated into English, I applied for a Fulbright Scholarship. The State University of San Diego had put me on their short list. The head of the Department of Romance Languages, Tom Cox, rang me one day to tell me that he was very sorry, but I hadn't been selected. Two weeks later he rang again, in the evening, very charming: hardly had their candidate, the well-known film specialist Michel Ciment, landed than he had decided to go back to Paris, unable to bear the idea of living in exile. How did I feel about coming? I accepted at once and after my arrival was subjected to close surveillance for fear that I too might skedaddle. I owed the position to my rival's discouragement and am grateful to him for it to this day. I spent delightful months there teaching the *Nouveau*

Roman, for me a simple extension of the Naturalist School, Comparative Literature and the History of Socialist Doctrine in the Department of Political Studies. My apartment looked out onto the beach, I was beside the Pacific Ocean, half an hour from Mexico, in an ideal climate, as favourable to work as to pleasure, I lived together with my students. It was there that I read, amongst other things and not without difficulty, the whole of *À la Recherche du Temps Perdu*, of which my father used to say, quoting Céline, that it was written 'in over-elaborate Franco-Yiddish.' My contact with the American way of life revived the appeal of the Hexagon. I never feel so French as when I'm in the United States.

My parents came to see me. They were delighted and my mother stayed on by herself with me for ten days or so. The contact with a foreign culture turned her back into a girl again. Since she couldn't drive, she walked round the streets, regularly getting lost. She rang me from a call-box:

'Where are you?'

'At a big crossroads.'

'What it's name?'

'In an avenue called *Stop at red light*.'

'What else?'

'Just a moment, let me have another look. Oh yes, *Left lane must turn left*.'

'Those are instructions to drivers, Maman. Now stop being silly. The street must have a name.'

'I can't see anything. I really am an idiot. Sorry, Pascal, but I'm completely lost.'

She did it deliberately, arguing in her low voice, exploiting her weakness. I would spend hours looking for her, GPS and mobiles didn't exist yet. Sometimes the police would call me and bring her back, blushing and confused, locked up like a thief in the barred compartment at the back of the van. Above my apartment in the block where I lived on Pacific Beach, there was a charming lady, Janis Glasgow, a professor in the French Department and a specialist on George Sand. When she was away I went to cat-sit for her, at around six in the evening. I had to feed her tomcat and comb it while playing a CD of Rimsky-Korsakov's *The Flight of the Bumble Bee*. I also had to perform a few dance steps for the excessively hairy and music-loving beast, whose mistress said it was the Californian reincarnation of Isadora Duncan. It responded to all this by purring voluptuously. My mother insisted on accompanying me for this little ceremony and I got her to dance a waltz with me before His Feline Majesty.

At home I was for a long time the little emperor around whom everything revolved. I grew up under the loving eye of my mother, I felt necessary, my life was not pointless. Sometimes her cosseting irritated me. To tease her I would say, 'You love me too much, let me breathe.'

But I didn't have the slightest desire to leave her, I did my homework in the kitchen, close to her. I set the table, helped her pick over the lentils, peel the carrots. We had invented a method of learning to spell: there was Baron Circumflex, Count Subjunctive, Princess Cedilla, Cardinal Speech-Marks. It is doubtless from that period that the vision of a loving couple derives that stayed with me for a long time: to snuggle up in your beloved's arms while holding out your own to the women who pass by. In the town I took piano lessons from a certain Mademoiselle Zay, the daughter, as I was to learn twenty years later, of Jean Zay who had been Minister of Education in the Front Populaire Government of 1936–38 and was assassinated by the Vichy militia in 1944. She was, as

I remember, a little lady, self-effacing and solitary, who was distressed by my lack of application. I begged her to teach me about jazz, she sent me back to Debussy, for her the acme of modernism. For each lesson my mother made huge roast-beef sandwiches that eliminated what little attentiveness I had. I would set off home, overfull and annoyed at having disappointed my teacher once again. And when I attempted the regional conservatoire examination, for which I prepared an easy sonata by Mozart, I failed in a crescendo of wrong notes. My mother was devastated. She had dreamt of a Dino Lupatti, what she got was a mawkish lump of a teenager. When, later on, I finally discovered the blues, boogie-woogie, swing, jazz, I felt like going to see that woman who was so patient, so sad, and saying, 'Right then, Madame, let's have a little jam session, shall we.'

Our house, in the suburbs of Lyons, was too vast for me; through the cellar it was open to the underworld of the earth's crust, through the attic to the demons of the roof. Even today I still dream about it as a haunted place: the evil spirits coming from above and below to carry me off, to tear me to pieces. In the evenings I often had to go down to the basement to stoke the coal-fired boiler and I was afraid of being attacked by the dormice teeming round the larder. We had something that is rare nowadays: a huge garden where my father had made a vegetable plot, an orchard and a rabbit hutch. We lived in the town as if we were out in the country, gathering beans, potatoes, carrots; I would weed the plot, feed the animals. In the summer I watered the plants and flowers before dinner: hydrangeas, petunias, hollyhocks, gladioli according to the season, adders and grass snakes fled under the jet from the pipe. But in the evening monsters came out of the ground and besieged the house. They were looking for me to kill me, I heard steps on the stairs, I screamed for help, fear was my most constant emotion. Whenever my father left on a trip, I went to sleep with my mother, at least until I was eleven or twelve. I had her all to myself, I didn't have to share her any more. I was a caricature of the Oedipus Complex: we were finally alone together, freed from Mr Moody. She would read to me, I remember *The Yearling* by Marjorie Kinnan Rawlings and other children's classics, A. J. Cronin, Jules Verne, Maurice Constantin-Weyer. I would go to sleep in her arms, sure that the world was a friendly place for me, that it was going to accept me. I wonder whether she too, when we slept together in that large house, didn't dream of finishing with my father. He'd done his duty in giving her a son. She would have had difficulty making ends meet but perhaps she would have met a more considerate man, found remunerative work, stood on her own two feet. If at that time she had suggested we bump him off, I would doubtless have accepted, so fed up was I with the loudmouth. But she went along with him, always finding, for all his disgraceful behaviour, mitigating circumstances for her tormentor, sharing more with him than I assumed. He killed her slowly but surely, she sacrificed herself to his moods instead of taking control of her destiny herself.

And just as he spent fifty years persecuting her, he looked after her with equal devotion during the last months of her life. Dying was the only revenge she could take on him, since she couldn't win him over. For years she had begged him to go on a diet because he weighed more than a hundred kilos, telling him he was digging his grave with his own teeth and that she didn't want to inherit his debts. He didn't even do her that favour. In our family it's the men that bury their wives. When she died and was in a cubicle in Cochin Hospital, I said to my father, 'It's you who should be in that box, not her. It's the best who go first.'

For years all the old ladies in the street took on my mother's face. It seemed that every one of them was giving me encouraging signs: 'Don't worry, I'm watching over you.'

I remember giving a talk in Rheims when one of my books came out. The room was more or less empty, the organiser full of apologies. Just the front row was taken with a group of old women, the regulars. Hardly had I opened my mouth than – so spellbinding was my discourse – they all fell asleep as one. Sometimes one of them would open her eyes, give me a smile then doze off again. But at the end these august residents of old folk's homes gave me rapturous applause. In each of those women dressed to the nines I thought I could see my mother, 'Well done, my son, keep it up, I'm proud of you.'

I invited her to come on a cruise with me, round the Mediterranean or to Egypt to see the Holy Places, the pyramids. For a long time she refused, afraid it might upset my father, and when she finally did accept, she was too ill to go. Right until the end I, together with my son, remained the principal object of her affection. I would sometimes see her in the Rue Montorgueil District, where I lived for a long time with my boy; she would wander round, do some shopping, hoping to run into one or other of us by chance. Half the time I would avoid her, not without a guilty conscience, knowing that the least encounter would lead to hours of advice, concerned remarks about how pale, how thin I looked, ending with the eternal question, 'I hope you're not doing anything stupid?'

'Oh but I am, Maman. It's only stupid things that are worthwhile in life.'

Every day, around the beginning of the afternoon, I find myself expecting her to call. It was a habit we'd got into and that weighed heavily on me at the time. That silence is like a splinter stuck in my heart.

Chapter 3

The Semitic Poison

We're in Mittelberg, Austria, during the 1956 Christmas holidays. I'm eight; we make a pilgrimage there every year. We're staying at *Kaffee Anna*, a few hundred metres from the *Kinderheim*, where I'm going to visit my old teachers. My German has already faded somewhat. It's lunch time. The waitresses in their frilly caps are serving dishes of sausages and cabbage, slices of venison with cranberries, soup with *knödel* (bread-and-potato dumplings), glasses of cherry schnapps. While we're waiting to sit down, I go to the toilets to clean myself up after skiing. A tall man in leather trousers and a Tyrolean hat is waiting for me to finish washing my hands. He gives me a good look and as I pass him says in strong local dialect, pointing his finger at me:

'*Du bist ein Jude.*' (You're a Jew.)

'*Nein, ich bin nicht.*' (No I'm not.)

'*Doch, doch, das kann ich sicher sagen.*' (Oh yes you are, I can say that with no doubt at all.)

I run off to tell my father what he said. He sees red, gets up and goes off to find the man, who's already left and taken a few steps on his way. My father addresses him, my mother fears there's going to be a scene. The two adults have a talk, I don't know what the word 'Jew' means, I just know it's something that's not good. My father waves to us, I'm to go out and join them. I obey as if I've done something stupid. Perhaps I've been insolent to the gentleman? My father makes me show my profile, from the left and from the right, points to my little nose with his index finger. It's only much later that I'll come to understand what's going on: he's giving the stranger a course in racial physiognomy. He's not blaming him for having insulted me but for having misread my face. His interpretation was wrong. That little nose isn't hooked like the Jews', at most it's aquiline. I come from pure Aryan stock. He all but takes my trousers down. The man apologises, pats me on the cheek and goes off. The gentleman is nostalgic for the old regime. For me there was no doubt that Austria in those days oozed hatred of the Jews and desire for revenge.

Both my mother's and father's families were bilingual from the cradle: we learnt antisemitism along with French. There was no animosity in it, it was just a fact of nature, like the law of gravity or the rotation of the Earth round the Sun. The war had done nothing to change this outlook inherited from the thirties and centuries of Christian anti-Judaism. On the contrary: it was because of the Jews that we had suffered all that misery, that carnage. They had dragged us into chaos with their strange customs and their passion for money. Thus the victims were made the cause of their own misfortune. In my father this mental reflex had reached extreme proportions. As far back as I can remember, from breakfast on he would do nothing but go on about the Yids, sheenies and other charming terms. He had never recovered from the defeat of the *Wehrmacht* and was consumed with eternal hatred for de Gaulle, the English, the Americans. Referring to the first of these in his war diary of 1941, he expressed his indignation that his comrades in the *Chantiers de Jeunesse*, a paramilitary organisation set up by the Vichy regime, listened to 'Mister Arsehole's long-winded speeches' on Radio London while he stuck stamps with the portrait of Marshal Pétain on every page. As he grew older this inclination determined his view of the world. Taken to such a degree of intensity, antisemitism is no longer an opinion but a passion informing the whole of one's being. Worse still, a passion that feeds on refutation. My father would read Jewish writers such as Léon Poliakov and Jules Isaac in order to find additional reasons for loathing the Jews. To see this detestation migrate from the European extreme right to the whole of the Arab-Muslim world – *The Protocols of the Elders of Zion* is sold on the streets of Cairo and in the bookshops of certain French mosques – filled him with amazement at the end of his life. Radical Islam, from the Muslim Brethren to the Salafi Movement via al-Quaida and Hezbollah, has become one of the repositories of the Nazi treasure.

Such strong loathing can either carry you along with it or repel you. Engaging as he was, my father might well have enlisted me on his side, at least for a few years, but it was his bellicose disposition that drove me to identify with those he abhorred. I would have liked to have met him when he was twenty, to have taken him in hand, saved him from getting stuck in certain ruts. All children dream of re-creating their parents, of putting them back on the right road. My mother would sing from the same score as him, though in the minor key; it was one of the places where they shared common ground, they made up on the backs of the 'Israelites', for her it was a way of diverting her husband's anger. 'You know it was the Jews who killed Jesus, Pascal.'

'Oh really. And is that serious?'

Every day we were treated to interminable disquisitions on Charles Maurras, Marshal Pétain, gentle Robert Brasillach and fiery Lucien Rebatet. He adored those last two, we had all their books in the house and every week my father would read the editorials Rebatet wrote for *Rivarol*, an extreme right-wing rag founded by Michel Dacier that denied the existence of Nazi gas chambers and for which ADG and Gérard de Villiers amongst others wrote. Our library was full of classics of the Collaboration: Thierry Maulnier rubbing shoulders with Tixier-Vignancourt, Maurice Bardèche, Benoist-Méchin, not to mention the works of Drumont and Céline – the latter a little too subversive for my progenitors. Rommel's memoirs were subjected to extensive commentary in the course of our meals, as were those of Jacques Isorni, the lawyer who defended Pétain, and of Henri Massis, who had put the finishing touches to Pétain's defence. Alexis Carrel, the father of eugenics, also occupied a prominent place. My parents had devoured Roger Peyrefitte's book *The Jews*. They appreciated the talented and provocative writer, the notorious braggart, even though they deplored his homosexuality. With the aim of demolishing antisemitism, he 'revealed' in his book that all the famous people of the time, de Gaulle, Kennedy, Brigitte Bardot, the Queen of England and even Hitler, were Jewish. My parents, sceptical, had drawn the opposite lesson from reading it: the Jews really were everywhere, under the camouflage of the most diverse identities. They had to be ever more vigilant. On the radio we listened to the harangues of M. Poujade,[3] his scathing

3 A populist right-wing politician.

attacks in the mid-fifties on Edgar Faure and the 'stateless minorities of dealers in stolen goods and homosexuals' that were ruining France.

In our family each tried to outdo the other in declaring that we had gone to war with Germany for 'those stupid Polacks' and with the defeat we'd been paid back in our own coin. Holidays with pay had ruined the country, the French had had too much fun, the *Épuration*[4] had been worse than the Occupation, the Allies had committed crimes as bad as those of the Germans. The atrocities of the ones cancelled out those of the others. Later on I came across the same arguments from Stalinist intellectuals who justified the mass murders of communism with those of capitalism. For my father there was nothing to the east of a line from Trieste to Danzig, going through Vienna, but subhumans, the Slavs, all equally turbulent and despicable, they too destined for extermination after the Jews and the gypsies. None found favour in his eyes, neither the Hungarians, nor the Romanians, nor the Albanians, the sole exception being the Czechs of the Sudeten because they spoke German. I listened to his imprecations without understanding them, perplexed and incapable of disentangling truth from falsehood, split between the desire to agree with him in order to please him or to take issue with it in order to assert myself.

'But what is it these Jews have done to you?'

'But…' he was stammering as he was so furious, 'but, well, it's obvious, isn't it? They've corrupted everything, defiled everything, trampled everything underfoot. They want to rule the world, they scoff at our most sacred values. The only Jews I like are those who are ashamed of being what they are.'

4 The 'legal purge', the series of trials of collaborationists, some condemned to death for treason, that followed the Liberation.

He thought for a moment, then went on, 'You see, you can't trust them. They're always on the move, one day here, the next day there. *Luftmenschen* as they say in German, creatures of the air. Moreover they're racists, they don't want to mix. I don't like their irony, they don't respect anything. Look at the Marx Brothers: I've always found their films unhealthy, tacky.'

It was a weak argument but its force lay precisely in its weakness. Animosity is based on ignorance of the original grievance. No longer remembering the reason for the animosity, we are happy to keep it going like a fire, by rekindling the embers.

Even today I still cannot understand the reasons for this phobia pushed to the extreme. The key perhaps lies in our origins: Huguenots expelled from south-eastern France, the Nîmes region to be precise, by Louis XIV's revocation of the Edict of Nantes, our ancestors took refuge in Germany and Austria, married Bruckners then settled in Aachen, Liège, Antwerp, Paris and Brussels. For two centuries they were constantly going to and fro between those countries, as their business took them. Our genealogy is the embodiment of the tensions in Franco-German relations: each generation choosing one camp against the other, siding with the one on top at the time. Although born a German subject, my great-grandfather Émile refused to speak German, comparing it to chewing straw. My grandfather, who spoke Dutch and loved all things German, volunteered for the Royal Belgian Army in 1914, spent four years at war and later described them as the best years of his life. After having fought against the *Boches*, he married an upper-middle-class German Jew, Frau Frankfurter, but divorced her soon after because she was sterile. A compulsive informer, he was said by my father to have denounced his own father as an agent of the *Kaiser*, that led to his parent having his goods confiscated and threatened with prison before he was rehabilitated. Then in the early nineteen-fifties my grandfather, after having been imprisoned for three months in 1944 on suspicion of collaboration – the whole of the Pas-de-Calais and Nord departments had been placed under the German Military Government of Belgium for the duration of the war – denounced his own son to the *Mines de la Sarre*, accusing him of having abandoned him and leaving him destitute. He turned up at the manager's office in rags as proof of his condition. After that he wrote to the head of the Jesuits in Lyons in order to defame me, describing me as a bad lot, unworthy of the teaching they provided. A dyed-in-the-wool Protestant, he couldn't bear the idea of me being educated in a papist institution. He was, as they said in the family, 'a queer fish', a mild euphemism they used for a perverse character who, on the other hand, was a talented water-colour artist and pianist. He loved to have a dig at people while playing the innocent. At dinner once, when he was visiting us in Lyons, he pointed at my mother and asked, completely out of the blue, 'Tell me, René my lad, who's that skinny woman eating with us?'

He would rummage through drawers, read letters and purloin them or tear them up if they happened to displease him.

My father repeated this Franco-German antagonism in his own way: in 1942, anticipating the Vichy *Service du Travail Obligatoire*[5] by several months, he went to work, first in Berlin, then in Vienna until the spring of 1945, for Siemens, which at the time supplied military equipment. Siemens paid the SS to have Jewish or Soviet slaves working for them.

---

5 STO: Compulsory Work Service that sent French workers as forced labour to Germany.

The prisoners were used in the programme of extermination by work until they were worn out. Thus he volunteered to serve Germany, putting his skills at the disposition of the *Reich* armaments industry. I found evidence of his activity in several Collaborationist newspapers in which he was proposing to train young technicians from France through the *Perfectionnement Technique des Travailleurs Français en Allemagne*,[6] as a section of the *Deutsche Arbeitsfront* with offices at 14 Grillparzerstrasse, Vienna. He retained fond memories of his three years in Berlin and Vienna. He would often tell me that it was the best part of his life, just as the Argonne trenches were for his father. If he had to do it again, he'd set off at once. In a sort of logbook, compiled in German and for which he collected train tickets, postcards and blades of grass, he records for example a visit to Berchtesgaden on 8 October 1944, noting the splendid view of the Königssee. The world was being torn apart by the war and he was taking a holiday by the Führer's Eagle's Nest in his free time. Or he notes an apparently convivial evening in the *Habsburghaus*, a Hitler Youth mountain hut at 2000m on the Rax Alp south of Vienna in October 1943. The anecdotal form of the diary is quite cleverly chosen: it covers him should he be arrested by either side. He could be accused neither of spying nor of ideological collusion. He had taken his brother Maurice with him; he was a handsome lad who was almost sent to the salt mines for having seduced an officer's wife.

In March 1945, with the Red Army at the gates of Vienna, my father fled with his girlfriend, a dyed-in-the-wool Nazi like himself, to hide in the Tyrol and Vorarlberg while waiting for things to settle down. I can imagine his flight from the

6 PTTFA: a scheme to improve the skills of French workers in Germany.

Russian troops, his wanderings on roads crowded with refugees, his nights in barns or isolated farmhouses, his fear of being informed on at any moment and handed over to the French troops arriving from the west, his stupefaction at the crushing defeat and the suicide of his idol in his bunker. Pierre Laval himself had been arrested in Innsbruck, that had been liberated by the local resistance, the *Österreichische Freiheitsfront*, in the summer of 1945, and handed over to the French authorities before being tried and executed. Then my father got to Hamburg where, by some piece of trickery that escapes me – had he seduced the young woman who looked after the registers at the French consulate? – he managed to get his name deleted from the lists of persons sought by the Liberation authorities.

He returned to France in the autumn of 1945, giving himself out to be a victim of the STO. This timorous man, who bowed before the least authority, was weak before the strong and pitiless when facing the weak, adored the savage brutality of certain bullies because he was incapable of it himself. Like Laval, who declared in 1942, 'I desire the victory of Germany,' he had put his money on the comprehensive triumph of the *Reich*. For him, as for my mother, the trauma of the defeat of 1940 was translated into unbounded admiration for the victor. 'You have crushed me, I adore you.' The *Blitzkrieg* and the German victory were so complete that they had to last for ever. No military power could neutralise them. Britain would go over to Berlin or be crushed, anyway the British were culturally and racially close to the Germans; as for the USA, they would remain neutral. The terrible chaos of the Exodus, the desperate flight of hundreds of thousands of civilians, fanned the flames of their anger at the Jews and the Freemasons, those significant factors in the outbreak of the war. Later on I came across this going over to the victor in the *Journal* of Drieu La Rochelle who went from idolising Hitler to doing the same for Stalin in the summer of 1944:

'Hitler's even more stupid than Napoleon (...) He arrived too late in a Europe too old and terribly shrunk (...) The Russians are approaching Warsaw. Hosanna! Hurrah! That's what I'm shouting today. Since the bourgeoisie's idiotic, Hitlerism's nothing but a happy medium (savage, like all happy mediums) since Europe refuses to acknowledge and join them, well then, let God's will be done, as the saying goes. Now I have faith in Stalin. Instinctively, I must add, I've always been for Stalin and against Trotsky: I'm always for the one who shoulders the heaviest responsibility.'[7]

At least Drieu La Rochelle was to have the courage to admit to his betrayal. Refusing Malraux' offers to hide him, he managed, after several attempts, to commit suicide with Gardenal in March 1945.

One morning, I must have been twelve, I had come down to breakfast in my pyjamas doing the goose step, keeping my legs straight as I swung them nice and high, emitting guttural sounds, very proud of my imitation. My father gave me a clip round the ear and I had to go to the kitchen. My mother came to console me, telling me my father had problems. He didn't like people mocking the Führer, he never forgave Charlie Chaplin for his film *The Great Dictator*. He had made a fatal diagnostic mistake. He had thrown himself enthusiastically into the arms of the Blond Beast and never disclaimed his choice. He never recovered from the German surrender of 8th and 9th

7 Pierre Drieu La Rochelle: *Journal 1939–1945*, Gallimard, introduced by Julien Hervier, 1992, pp. 408 & 416.

May 1945, that he attributed to a Judaeo-Bolshevik plot: the Jews acting in the garb of both Anglo-Saxon capitalism and Soviet communism. If he managed to conceal his resentment in public – he used to say that international Jewry put a curb on his mouth – he made up for it in private. It was like a verbal purge, a cesspool of words he emptied over us. It could pour out at any moment. He had to express his aversion to them every day. But the cesspool was never completely emptied. His Nazism, largely imaginary, found expression in a verbal itch, a kind of posture adopted for the sake of it. Even at the height of the conflict he had never been more than an insignificant spectator. I asked him to tell me if he had ever spilt blood – he had boasted of having been to Dachau several times. He swore that he hadn't. Do I dare admit it? I was disappointed, I would have preferred a real torturer to an underling. In this, too, fate has refused me the possibility of greatness in abhorrence. I would have found a torturer loathsome, with no saving grace. But can one abominate a mediocrity?A few months before his death, in 2012, he told me that my mother had also gone to work for Siemens in Germany, starting in the winter of 1940. But she came back quickly, incapable of mastering German. Full of remorse and even horrified, she'd made him swear never to tell me. This little secret moves me: my mother had felt ashamed and that saves her in my eyes.

I described my father in my novel of 1981 *Lunes de fiel* (translated as *Evil Angels*) in the person of an old fascist who was dying and swapped his hatred of the Jews for that of the Arabs. He liked the book, the only one of my novels he was happy to read and he wasn't offended by the allusion. I had been mistaken: his hatred of the Jews was non-negotiable, he preferred it to all others. They remain the best in the large range of scapegoats. They can boast a tradition going back two thousand years. With the Arabs it would eventually be possible, once certain misunderstandings had been cleared out of the way, to make an alliance against the sons of Judah. Those he could spot anywhere, behind even the most anodyne surname. He would sniff surnames with a Germanic component, chew them over, repeat them, take them to pieces, until they gave off, as he put it, 'a whiff of the *shtetl*.' As a child I swam in a linguistic pool that has been largely forgotten nowadays: sheeny, wop, dago, levantine, thug, touch of the tarbrush, wog. My son and I used to laugh at these invectives as the ramblings of a senile dotard. Even today we still repeat some of his assertions like pieces from an anthology. In a certain way I've always viewed my father's political opinions as belonging to folklore. I didn't grasp their true significance until much, much later. When friends of mine came to the house I would warn them, fearing some ill-chosen remark from my father, about his 'slightly odd' ideas. I did it in the way you'd talk about an eccentric or incontinent old uncle who was not to be taken seriously. It was my own way of setting up a shield of derision between him and myself. Real family secrets are not those you keep quiet about but the ones that are known to everyone. Overexposed and therefore inaudible.

I used to bombard him with books on the Nazis and their crimes, and for his ninetieth birthday I gave him a book on the Führer by the English historian, Ian Kershaw. He didn't read it, obviously, but after having leafed through it, he said, 'What an idiot that Hitler was! He was so stupid. He should have waited for the end of the war to resolve the Jewish question. First of all defeat the Russians and the Allies with the V2, then have a clear-out. Commandeering thousands of trains to transport them to the camps, what a waste of time! Mark you, he didn't need to exterminate them. He could have packed them off to

Madagascar or central Asia. He could have sealed the frontiers hermetically to make sure no Jew could escape. There were other solutions… I have a theory, you know. Listen closely to what I'm going to say, it may well be confirmed by historians one day: Hitler was deceived by the party officials. Göring, or Himmler perhaps. They were the real bastards. In fact, Hitler wasn't a Nazi.'

Another time when I went to see him at Sainte-Marie Hospital, right at the end, I could hear his telephone conversation with his last 'girlfriend' – a mistress from his young days, an upper-middle-class lady and, like him, a belated sympathiser with National Socialism – while I was still out in the corridor: 'The guy who does the tests on me here's called Gluckstein, right. Need I say more?'

Their love of Germany was such that, when they were alone together they talked to each other, with their quavering voices, in an antiquated *Hochdeutsch*, the language of the master race; it was strange to hear them producing the syllables with a French accentuation. It was like a fragment of the past cut out of its time and inserted just as it was in the present.

One day, around 2005, my father called me. He was furious. He'd just received a letter from the Austrian Foreign Ministry, the BMeiA (*Bundesministerium für europäische und internationale Angelegenheiten*), offering him compensation for his 'years of captivity'. The sum could be backdated, if he so wished. He was almost speechless with rage.

'I sent them a strong letter telling them how proud I was to have served at Siemens. Repudiating their history like that – they ought to be ashamed of themselves.'

When he really got on my nerves, I would ask him why he hadn't joined the Resistance. Quite a few men from the extreme right, like Colonel de La Rocque, who was deported to Czechoslovakia and to Austria, or Daniel Cordier, alias Caracalla, had gone underground and fought bravely. His indignation knew no bounds: the Resistance fighters were assassins, ex-convicts, people who refused to do their duty and go and work in Germany – apart from the men of the *Maquis des Glières* who had paid with their lives for their stupidity, having been abandoned by 'that shit de Gaulle and those English bastards'. His opinion of the General was what Drieu la Rochelle had written in his *Journal* entry of 12th January 1944:

'De Gaulle is a master of ceremonies hired by the Jews to add lustre to their return to France. The Jews love the noble "de".'[8]

He greeted May '68 with suspicious elation, at least during the first weeks. It did him good to see his worst enemy pilloried as Hitler on the posters in the street: the traitor was finally being forced to eat dirt. He even had a liking for the fanatical German Jew, Daniel Cohn-Bendit.

During the war in Algeria there was a file on him as an OAS[9] sympathiser; at least that was what he claimed, perhaps he was just boasting. On a day when de Gaulle, on an official visit to Lyons, was to pass our house, the police came to search and occupy the property. The only courageous act he allowed himself was to shout 'Dirty rotten traitor!' as the presidential cortège passed. I watched him ranting and raving while the police looked on good-naturedly. My mother, embarrassed, had remained hidden inside the house. It was the failure of the Petit-Clamart attempted assassination of

8 *Journal*, op. cit., p. 360.

9 *Organisation de l'Armée Secrète:* an extreme right-wing paramilitary organisation during the Algerian war.

de Gaulle in August 1962, but above all the execution of the main instigator of the plot, Colonel Bastien-Thiry, shot by firing squad on 11th March 1963, that put the final touch to the aversion my father had had for the General since 18th June 1940. He was to dance for joy and break out the champagne on the day he died, 9th November 1970.

I can see my father in a photo with me in the Kleinwalsertal in 1951. I'm wearing a Tyrolean skullcap, a sort of little embroidered saucer, and a baggy romper-suit pulled in with elastic round the thighs. He's handsome, slim, with grey-blue eyes and a full head of hair. Six years previously he'd escaped being shamed as a traitor by the skin of his teeth. He could have made a fresh start on new foundations, buried his aberration in his memory. Who would have suspected that this elegant man regularly wallowed in obscene orgies and shameful nostalgia? For a long time I had hoped that he was a kind of Binjamin Wilkomirski of the Collaboration, after the Swiss manufacturer of musical instruments who in the 1990s had given himself out to be a survivor of the Holocaust: a sham collaborator hiding his courage behind outrageous assertions, a sort of double agent of the Resistance. He could have fooled us all only to reveal himself, in the evening of his days, bathed in the glory of the secret *tzaddik*. Every time television, radio or the newspapers brought up the events of 1940–1945 again, he would fume, 'How long are they going to keep on pissing us off with their genocide crap?'

He never managed to change his ways, he continued to be in thrall to the Nazi Moloch. Contemporary France was not the natural development of the Second World War, that remained for him the absolute yardstick, his Freudian family romance. The scars hadn't healed over, the animosity resurfaced at every crisis, especially when Berlin outperformed Paris economically, reopening the wounds of over a hundred years of defeat: three wars with two debacles – two and a half if one remembers that the victory of 1914–18 was only gained at the price of an unprecedented loss of life and thanks to the Allies' final push. Faced with her powerful eastern neighbour, France suffers from a defeatist complex. She has never recovered from those four years of humiliation, whereas the end of her colonial empire was a relief to the majority of the population. It isn't Islam or immigration that is weakening us, they are merely symptoms revealing our weakness, but our nation has long borne the stigmata of the collapse and of Vichy. Current events are all viewed from that perspective: each of the political factions accuses the others of collaborating with Evil and that includes the extreme right that presents itself as embodying resistance to the foreign invasion. On television in 2013 a Professor Nimbus even expressed the suspicion that German industry wanted to 'exterminate' (sic!) French industry. This stupid attitude has even infected the younger generations: the anarchists march past singing the '*Chant des partisans*' (the battle hymn of the Resistance), the Islamists compare their fate to that of the Jews during the war, the ethnic groups call the CRS the SS, the accusation of collaborationism or Pétainism is widespread in all factions. We are endlessly replaying the Occupation. What I hold against my father is that he ruined German culture for me. I automatically deleted the language from my memory because it was his, choosing in its place English, that allows you to feel at home in the most far-off places, puts you on an equal footing with all people. My father justified Hitler in the light of Mozart and Beethoven, deriving the former from the other two by the mere fact of cultural proximity. *The Third Reich* proceeded to the trills of

The Magic Flute, the oompahs of the *Ode to Joy*. A culture that had produced such masterpieces couldn't be completely bad, especially when they played great music in the huts of the concentration camps. That an executioner can be a music lover does make you think despite everything. On Saturdays and Sundays at home we were treated to *Deutschland über alles*, the German national anthem taken from a string quartet by Haydn, who adapted it from a Croatian tune, never Mahler or Mendelssohn. I was to find it impossible to bear listening to classical music until I was forty.

Fortunately the family library contained English and American books as well, mostly bought by my mother, from Katherine Mansfield to Charles Morgan, Dickens, Faulkner, Dos Passos and D. H. Lawrence. It was during that period that I made Anglo-Saxon culture my second homeland. I haven't changed since.

During the time of his relative prosperity my father had a period of remission. He started to prefer the Austro-Hungarian Empire, as a model of tolerance and of coexistence between minorities, to *The Third Reich*. He read a large number of Austrian or Hungarian Jewish authors – Joseph Roth, Franz Werfel, Sándor Marai – and developed liberal theories on the question. I thought he was cured of his obsessions but they'd just changed direction. He became a philosemite and that was the worst of all. From an accursed nation, the Jews were suddenly raised to the status of a model nation endowed with all the virtues. They showed us the way. His revulsion turned into envy. They were polyglot, they could begin a sentence in German, carry on in English and complete it in Russian or French. They all spoke *Emigranto*, picked up any language whatsoever in a few months. They were rich, supported each other, were united. A Jew from Odessa had relatives in Argentina, in South Africa, in China. When times were hard none were left outside, they understood each other, helped each other. That was the little speech that, proud of his broadmindedness, he served up to Alain Finkielkraut when he came to lunch with us. After we left university, Alain and I had developed a very close friendship and written two books together. We were two only sons in search of a spiritual twin, he the child of a man deported to Auschwitz, I of a National-Socialist sympathiser. The conversation over the meal was courteous but cool.

'If it hadn't been for you, I would have got up and left,' Alain told me, appalled. 'I was treated to all the anti-Semitic commonplaces of the thirties.'

My father, for his part, found my friend well-brought-up but 'narrow-minded'. He really would never be able to understand 'those people'. But subsequently he would always spring to his defence, in the name of our friendship, just as he was to be unwavering in his admiration for Roman Polanski for having adapted one of my novels. This liberal period lasted for several years but his natural disposition reasserted itself with his first setbacks. Added to that, the fact that when I was forty I became part of the family of Gérard Oury (real name Tannenbaum), established very close and lasting ties with each of them, became immersed in the womb-like warmth of the tribe and had a child, Anna, with his granddaughter Caroline Thompson, sparked off violent feelings of jealousy in him. The 'Jews' had stolen his son, had corrupted him with their comfortable lifestyle, with their money. I was moving from a society of mutual humiliation to a circle of mutual admiration where each would compliment the other to raise the level of esteem of the group as a whole. The generous use of the superlative was a relief for me after his unlimited recourse to disparagement. And when my partner and I separated sixteen years later, his only comment was, 'Just you watch out, the Jews always take their revenge…'

He had an explanation for everything. I regarded him as seriously ill. The culmination of his mania came several years later in a comment to my son: 'Your father's the only person who's managed to con the Jews. I've no idea how he did it.'

Part Two

The Great Escape

Chapter 4

The Glorious Taste of the Outside World

How can we escape from our childhood? By rebelling and fleeing, but above all by attraction: by multiplying the passions that push us out into the world. Freedom is to increase the number of things we're dependent on, servitude to be restricted to ourselves. I lightened the burden my family imposed on me by weighing myself down with other ties that have enriched me. Before even emitting a sound, we're talked about by our parents, a passive object of their speculations. Then, despite themselves, they draw up the constitution of our existence, attributing to us a certain taste, a certain profession, projecting their own desires onto their descendants. At fourteen I had a terrible feeling of being trapped; my life had hardly begun and was already finished. I started to write so as not to become a story written by my family. I was threatened with an insidious but irrevocable disaster: mediocrity. Like everyone who's defenceless, I dreamt of being all-powerful. Initially I used lies to protect myself. I made myself a shield out of fictions,

I found myself concocting cock-and-bull stories like a jazz musician improvising riffs. They pretended to believe me. A good lie has to be based on elements of truth, it has to seem likely. One day my system backfired on me – the moment came, as it always does, when the storyteller got tangled up in the tissue of lies he'd woven. Lying becomes a good reason not to change anything in your life unless it's an act designed not to reflect the past but to determine the future. I've retained my propensity to embroider everything so as to give the fabric of my days a more romantic sheen. I continue to subject the facts to a process of exaggeration that, in return, forces me to make my life conform to the account I've given of it. I make up stories in order to haul myself up to their level.

I begged my parents to send me to boarding school. They tried to enrol me for the Jesuit College in Fribourg, Switzerland, where teaching was trilingual. I was rejected: my faith had gone, I had moved from sanctimony to mockery, I was violently anticlerical, I was the leading light of an atheist circle at the Jesuit school in Lyons and my bad reputation had preceded me. The Fathers were clever: they tolerated an anticlerical challenge in their midst while reminding us, 'You may not believe in God, but God still believes in you.' I think that above all the fees in Swiss francs were too high for the family budget. I was growing, I was starting to confront my father directly. Several times we'd almost come to blows, I was fuming, I was dying to hit him. He would bawl, I would bawl even louder and, without realising, I was beginning to sound like him. He threatened to send me to a reformatory. I would reply, 'Great! Anything rather than vegetate in this dump.'

He wouldn't go that far, as I very well knew, it would be too damaging to his reputation. What he would have really liked would have been to have the right of life and death over me, like a lord under the *ancien régime*. Beatings were now a thing of the past for me, as were thrashings with the whip and the belt; I was simply too big. I had cut the cords off the first cat-o'-nine-tails my parents bought from the pharmacy in order to make them unusable, or I went and buried them in the garden. One night I dreamt that the whips, buried under the soil, had started to proliferate, like carrots or turnips, and that they were springing up everywhere, brand new and with cords furnished with painful balls of lead. All my cousins received thrashings with the cat-o'-nine-tails, it was customary at the time, as was being hit on the fingers with a ruler. Mostly it was enough just to show the whip to obtain obedience. On some evenings, when my father came home from work in a bad mood he needed to take it out on someone; if I should appear round a corner in the corridor, running too quickly or shouting too loud, he would give me a clout. Not for any particular reason, just to calm himself down. At table, if I responded to some comment or upset my plate, I received a double ration on both cheeks, one from my mother, one from my father. I had to leave the table and go to my room. Cheeks stinging, I would cry, repeating, 'I hate them, I hate them.' As time passed it was they who hurt themselves or twisted their wrist when they hit me. I burst out laughing every time. Corporal punishment is a minor matter as long as it doesn't turn into torture. You become inured to it, your skin gets tougher. When the whip stings your thighs, the cut from the lash turns into heat, leaving reddish streaks, as if from a cat's claws – marks of valour to show off to your friends. The real wounds are verbal, the negative judgments, the humiliations that imprint themselves on you in letters of fire. My father was absolutely determined to persuade me that I was inferior: I would end up as a down-and-out, an idler, a failure, unfit for work. Whenever I appeared he would survey me with a look of disapproval. Our struggle was fought out over the matter of haircuts, the capillary rebellion being one of the great leitmotifs of my generation: whenever my hair was more than a few centimetres long I had to go off to the barber, who would give my head a close shave. I was guilty before I'd even done anything and I would systematically make the error that would confirm my guilt: if he gave me a knife, warning me not to cut myself with it, I would immediately gash my finger.

There were also moments of truce when we all laid down our arms and forgot our grievances. For example, every Thursday we used to listen to *Les maîtres du mystère* on the radio: this was a crime series broadcast at dinner time with a theme tune, a kind of fearsome power saw rising to a crescendo, that sent shivers down our spines. The murder accompanied our first course, the solution came with dessert. In between we argued furiously about it, especially during the musical interludes. I would declare I knew who the culprit was, then retract, the others would contradict me; in general we were all wrong and the conclusion came as a surprise that left us flabbergasted.

For a child his father is a giant who shrinks as he grows. Like many only sons, I used to dream that one day an elegant man would knock at the door and, announcing that he was my true father, take me away from my family. I would dream of being carried off, imagine I was of noble birth and had fallen by chance into this milieu that didn't correspond to my aspirations. Even today I sometimes imagine a young man or woman ringing at my door and introducing himself as one of my children, the offspring of a fleeting encounter. I will welcome him or her in the name of something I've always prized highly: the fruitfulness of the unexpected. My father behaved in an authoritarian manner without exercising real authority. Added to the terror a despot can inspire is the disappointment at finding him vulnerable. The awareness of his lack of consistency made the ground give way under my feet. His racist aberrations did nothing to help him in life: the man who had kept us down for so many years, the operetta *Gauleiter* who exploded at the least annoyance, would bow and scrape to his superiors. This is the mechanism of indirect transmission: every teacher, lecturer, head of state is permanently presenting two contradictory attitudes. There is what his lips are uttering and what his body is suggesting. When the latter contradicts the former it arouses confusion in the child, the pupil or the citizen. The brutality, the scorn or the fear that emerge from a certain body language can nullify the sense of what the words are saying.

With adolescence I started to write in order to imitate the authors I admired, to get my life moving, to escape from the common lot. I covered pages with violent or grotesque stories. I became a writer in order to be loved, redeemed from the sin of existing. At that time I made an absurd vow: I will not get married, I will not have children, I will never work. I only, thank heavens, kept the last part of this resolve, having lived from my books for the past forty years, thus avoiding the servitude of paid labour. Between the age of thirteen and sixteen I discovered a principle stronger than revolt: the principle of exteriority. Our motivations do not reside in the resentment that keeps us tied to the object of our loathing. Beyond that an unconditional acceptance of life is essential. There is a richer, denser world outside the family circle. To families I say, I neither love you nor hate you – I leave you on one side.

At the Jesuits' school, immersed in a milieu that was neither harsh nor benign, I distinguished myself by being better at my work than the others. Study was the fast track to emancipation. I won all the prizes, I was the unbearable model pupil. Lyons in the sixties was a grey city with no relation to the Italianate metropolis it has become today. The centre of a bourgeoisie in decline – that of the silk manufacturers ruined by the competition of other fibres, rayon and nylon – it had long been kept alive by the antagonism between the radical mayor, Edouard Herriot, a rabid anticlerical, and Cardinal Gerlier, Primate of Gaul and former Pétainist who became a saviour of Jewish children, and it stank of grime and provincialism. In the Ainay district, where my day school, St Joseph's, was situated, the streets were full of crows, as we called them, that is priests in their cassocks. As they passed we would shout, 'Caw, caw.' Among them there was, as I've already emphasised, the clerical proletariat, the minor priests, underpaid, underfed, with dirty, patched clothes, veritable beasts of burden. Their cassocks stank to high heaven, especially during hot weather, the servants of God having abandoned the use of soap. Our hatred of the Catholic school knew no bounds and, unable to insult the supervisors or the Superior, we took it out on their underlings. I would be furious at the memory of how, from the first years at the free school, fanatical mistresses, virtuous and dried-up old spinsters, would brandish their crucifixes and tell us we'd go to hell if we ate meat on a Friday. We would listen to them, terrified, and beg our parents to cook fish on that day. Later on my hatred of them was commensurate with the fear they had caused me. We were young horses who were champing at the bit. A child isn't meek and mild, it's just weak and hasn't yet had the chance to show its nastiness. In the refectory the meals were served by men who were moderately mentally handicapped that the Order employed for peanuts.

We used to bombard them with lumps of cream cheese, spinach, mashed potato until the supervisor came and ordered us to show some Christian charity. We never learnt: the others used to call me a 'filthy *Kraut*' and I would reply with 'filthy bastard,' it was all pretty primitive, we'd come to blows over nothing.

The Jesuits were excellent teachers. The education they provided was first rate, especially in the humanities and some of the staff were outstanding, in particular the philosophy teacher, Yves de Gentil-Baichy, later unfrocked, who introduced us to Kierkegaard, Jaspers, Gabriel Marcel, while we were being suffocated by Péguy, Bernanos, Léon Bloy, the officially recognised Christian thinkers of the time. In other respects they formed a pretty strict hierarchical organisation that hushed up any scandals, priests who touched up boys (fairly rare), lecherous confessors who got their parishioners pregnant and whose children the school took charge of without always being able to conceal their origin. With a Huguenot father and a papist mother, I ended up an agnostic. But ex-Christian atheists are not the same as ex-Islamic or ex-Jewish ones. They remain imbued with the very thing they repudiate, remaining Christians even in their refusal to acknowledge Christ. Even today, when I hear the bells of the nearby Armenian church in my apartment in the centre of Paris, where it's quieter than out in the country, I'm overcome with a feeling of peacefulness. There is nothing sweeter than a great religion in its twilight years, when it has renounced violence and proselytism and gives forth nothing but its spiritual message: faith transmuted into an aesthetic emotion, a nostalgia for childhood.

May '68 was to give post-war France a good shake-up, sweep away taboos that were already worm-ridden and only needed a puff of wind to blow them down. We baby boomers were fortune's children of the 20th century. We lived through the thirty glorious years after the Second World War, years of an unheard-of increase in disposable income, of unbridled sexual freedom unhindered by any fatal disease. It is impossible to overpraise the beauty of those blissful years, all entirely devoted to the celebration of desire and of youth, shot through with incredible artistic creativity. What a contrast to our present, locked in a culture of moaning and groaning. In the course of a single life we've seen the last convulsions of the patriarchal order, the liberation of morals and of women, the fall of communism, the collapse of Third-Worldism and now that of Europe, dying from its own triumph, from its guilty conscience. My intuition, going back to 1983 and *The Tears of the White Man*, of a Western society out of sorts with itself and cultivating self-doubt that kills, is being confirmed with every day that passes. To hate oneself is to prepare the way for one's own disappearance and France will manage that pretty soon. A whole group of our elites wants Europe to commit suicide or at least be obliterated to expiate our crimes of the past. To withdraw from the world, to quit history, that is our ideal. But it is us who are fading away while other nations are waking up.

With adolescence I felt I was at the dawn of a new life that was beckoning me to join it. I recall my rapturous response to hearing the voice of Aretha Franklin for the first time, on the juke box of a seedy Place Bellecour café. I was thunderstruck by the sumptuousness of her voice, a prodigality of breaths and scales, a near-perfection of *tessitura*. I felt as if I were being lifted off the ground, freed from the ties of gravity, and listened to the same song ten, a hundred times over. I was to buy all her recordings in all available media. That moment marked the start of my love of Afro-American music – gospel, blues, jazz, soul, funk – that has never failed and that I have passed on to my children.

At night I also used to listen, on a short-wave transistor radio, to Arab music that was forbidden at home; I was crazy about Oum Kalsoum, Farid al Atrash, Fairuz, Asmahan. It was the age of the twist, of *scoubidou*, those little, vaguely phallic plastic tubes named after a song sung by Sacha Distel, that could be twisted into all sorts of shapes, of the hula-hoop, the swaying hips of emancipation. Expressions that have now gone out of fashion flourished: *c'est bath* for *c'est bien* or *t'es plus dans le coup, papa* (you're not with it, granddad). *Sympa* and *génial* burst into the dictionary, with a great future ahead of them until they were usurped by 'fun' and 'cool'. Liberation arrived in the guise of agreeable infantilism, an immediate effusion of whims. Certain minor pleasures were regarded as insignificant and were therefore permitted at home. I secretly devoured bad films, an outlet for my frustration; my emotional poverty, my timidity were such that I saw mediocre writers as major authors, I could go on at length about the latest pop songs, the least novelette could give rise to fervent exegesis. On a Spanish beach an older boy explained Freud's *Three Essays on the Theory of Sexuality* to me and it made me dizzy. A whole continent was opening up before me. For want of anything else, I made do with my school-friends and we developed an eroticism of virgins consisting of mutual masturbation that didn't commit us to anything further but provided temporary relief. We would grope each other mechanically, without foreplay or fuss, anywhere we happened to be, in the study room, in the refectory, even in the sacristy; the semen would quickly spurt out and we would get dressed again. Some went a little farther, offering their mouths as a haven for our youthful lust. We despised them but availed ourselves of their services with the greatest discretion. One final-year boy called it 'the spermatic host' and we were fascinated by the sacrilegious term. Even today millions of adolescents start out on their sexual career by this roundabout route and then erase it from their memory later on. What is needed at that age is unbridled licentiousness using all available means: the urge is more important than the object, the libido is a river in spate.

From books, finally, I learnt the grammar of freedom thanks to the idols of my youth, Sartre, Gide, Malraux, Michaux, Queneau, Breton, Camus. Through them I constructed an impregnable fortress. We had no television, which turned out to be a piece of good luck: I was forced to read books and by exercising my imagination avoided the stupor of being drowned in the mishmash of visual images. The library was a bastion and a weapon, it protected me from the world and supplied me with arguments to confront it. I was at the age when you grab hold of a few giants you imagine you understand but in fact get wrong. At least they've opened up your mind, invited you to come back and see them again. I have never been disappointed by books, I've read a lot of poor ones but so many that are very good. Today I still buy some every week, happy to see them in such abundance, such profusion, even though I know it would take a hundred lives to read them all. I tremble as I open them, I'm looking for a revelation such as you might find in the body of a woman you've never met before, moved to find things you already know yet will never know. With each volume I go out of myself for a while, take up a different life, raise myself to another level of intelligence.

I was fourteen and a large poster on the walls of my room proclaimed, 'Neither god nor master'. Furious, my father had torn it down, just as he tore up the manuscripts I scribbled and, so he claimed, as he had torn a cross of Lorraine, a souvenir of a passing love affair, from round his sister's neck at the end of 1945, snarling, 'Take that filthy thing off!'

As I approached fifteen I ran away several times, to demonstrate my independence. It was pathetic; I never went very far, a few hundred kilometres at most, I left in order to return, to make my parents panic, just managing to avoid the police. One evening, refusing to go to the barber's, I boarded a night train to Paris at Lyon-Perrache Station. We were crammed into the second-class compartment, the third class having been abolished not long previously: one ecclesiastic, two soldiers, several rustics and a well-built, gaudily dressed young woman in a red velvet gown and a flowery hat. She was like a bar of soap wrapped in shiny skin. I sat down beside her, she couldn't have been more than ten years older than me and, in the middle of the night, she allowed me to rest my head on her shoulder.

She twittered, 'You'd like to give me a kiss, wouldn't you, you little rascal, but you're just a kid.'

The night-light bathed the compartment in a pale, mauve glow. The soldiers, young themselves, stared at us, wanting to join in the fun, furious that a young puppy should steal the prey they had their eye on. When they finally fell asleep, my plumed neighbour allowed me to explore her treasures while she pretended to be in a deep sleep. With delight I lost myself in the labyrinthine curves of her imposing body, trying to find my way by touch. We said goodbye the next morning on the platform of the Gare de Lyon, dishevelled and smiling. She allowed me to kiss her on the cheeks and gave me an affectionate slap to punish me for my boldness. Every time I've been threatened with misfortune, a woman's kindness has saved me.

A bold explorer early on – at eight an aunt found me with

my head between a female cousin's legs and sent me away with a box round the ears – I was almost eighteen before I went the whole way. At the time, faced with any woman at all, I would tell myself: it's beyond me and I would run off with my tail between my legs. To touch a woman's heart seemed such an achievement that I felt like a hero when I managed to get a kiss. I kept telling myself: if she agrees to hold my hand it will be such a triumph that I should prostrate myself in the dust. I would remain tongue-tied, awkward, incapable of expressing my emotions, the attraction I felt. I didn't know how to gain access to these unattainable fortresses. If I'd been more on the ball I would have been able to elude the family surveillance, find a way round the prohibitions and experience precocious delight. I got friends to tell me daring expressions that I learnt off by heart and repeated like a parrot. In brief, I misused those uncompleted loves of our youth, where you alternate between humility and scorn, and there was still within me something of the nastiness of little boys who are incapable of amusing themselves without ill-treating some being. As an adolescent you see love as a process of domestication of novelty; you don't know that to love is to allow the other person to detach themself from you and find the right distance to blossom. I was as inhibited as I was obsessed, especially since my mother, in alliance with my father this time, was keeping a weather-eye open. No young lady was allowed to cross our threshold without first having been examined by my mother – who would subject her to a pitiless interrogation – and given her stamp of approval. At any moment she was likely to burst into my first-floor bedroom in Lyons to check that we weren't taking advantage of our freedom to 'commit improprieties'. One day she told me, in veiled terms, what a disappointment her wedding night had been, the embarrassment of nudity, the dubious entanglements, the ugliness of the organs, hardly mitigated by the hope of having a child. From what she said, two weeks before their marriage my father had been summoned (alone) to a doctor, who explained to him the mysteries of the female body and of mutual fulfilment. He was charged with passing this information on to his future wife, who had not been judged worthy of being summoned. I just hope, for her sake alone, that she wasn't a virgin when she got married! For women of her generation marital duties were primarily a humiliation, rarely followed by pleasure. Her life ended, as it had begun, bathed in holy water; she spent her last years at Notre Dame, madly in love with Cardinal Lustiger, whose sermons she never missed.

A further episode determined my inclinations. I was spending the Easter holidays at La Clusaz with some other students, including my friend Laurent Aublin, who was in the same dormitory as me at the Lycée Henri Quatre. We met two sisters of sixteen and seventeen, we weren't much older. I flirted with the younger one, a pretty blonde who invited me to go and say goodbye to her in the hostel on the edge of the village where she was staying. Around one in the morning we went into a dormitory with some thirty beds. Holding me by the hand and not making a sound, my girlfriend led me to hers. There was a low exchange of soft snores, alternating with occasional sniffs or sighs. From the upper bunks there were arms hanging down in tragic style, inanimate legs shrouded in socks. The presence of a boy in the dormitory woke the sleepers. We clasped each other like clumsy children, trying everything without achieving anything at all. She allowed me many things but permitted nothing. In the silence our kisses, our caresses sounded like the rumble of thunder: we were being watched. The mattresses creaked, bodies turned over and over, and the little convent of sleep turned into a rustling hive. Our unfinished embrace had whetted unsuspected appetites in each of us. At dawn my sweet friend was hungry and started to devour a bag of pralines. Her jaws were crunching in my ear – I would have liked to be the sugared almond she was grinding between her teeth, go all the way down her oesophagus, sail along her veins, contribute to the growth of her magnificent body.

Towards six in the morning she chucked me out, the supervisors were about to arrive. I left by the window, climbed down a kind of drainpipe to retrieve my bag and shoes at the bottom. Across the valley the sun was rising over the Aravis range in glorious consecration of my night. A security guard nabbed me while I was still getting dressed, I gave him a smile to mollify him; happiness must have been written all over my face, he regarded me enviously, just as nowadays I envy the sybarites, the bright young things that go out at night to have a good time. I'm not of a jealous nature, more concerned with my own independence than with others' possible loose living. But to know that others are having fun while I'm bored stiff really gets my goat. The man let me go and I got a bus to Annecy Station. I had kept the girl's smell on my fingers, I was intoxicated by the delicious opium of her stomach and decided to keep it for as long as possible on the pad of my forefinger. I kept sniffing the nectar all the time.

In Lyons my mother welcomed me with suspicious looks. I was supposed to get back the previous evening.

'You're very ill, you know. If you go round doing just anything, you're risking the worst.'

I gave her an ironic look, my decision was taken: I'm going to devote my life to the glories of the female body.

I'm twenty-four or twenty-five and on the Paris-Marseille

Express at the height of summer. A woman of around thirty, suntanned, a typical brunette, in a short skirt, gets on at Lyons and sits opposite me in the compartment. I can't take my eyes off her legs all the way to Valence. At one point she uncrosses them and, overwhelmed, I think I catch a glimpse of the pink flash of panties. She's amused by my reaction and when we're passing through Orange she smiles, gets up, goes out into the corridor and leans on her elbows at the window. The train stops at every station. I go out, stand next to her and, imperceptibly, slide my fingers onto hers. She asks me what I'm playing at and I say it's not a game. We go to the little section joining the carriages, I grasp her arms and we kiss. My own boldness makes me choke. I want to take her into the toilet, she refuses, wants to know my Christian name first, I learn that she's going to join her husband and children on the Riviera. She allows me to take a few liberties, enough for me to tell she's aroused but not much more. In her fine Marseilles accent she explains that it would be too quick, too wham-bam-thank-you-ma'am. I have to rush to get off in Avignon where my parents and my son, a little boy, are waiting to meet me. I'm struck by the impropriety of the situation. Once more I feel caught in the family net. Whatever your age, your position, your parents have the knack of grabbing you by the collar and reminding you that for them you have been and always will be a helpless snotty-nosed little kid. Sexuality gives young men an illusory sense of superiority. But when it's only just taking shape, it pushes you back into your wretched state. On the platform I turn round and say goodbye to the passenger, I'm touched by the favours she granted me, sad to leave her. Our impromptu encounter had been spoilt by another refusal: she wouldn't give me her telephone number. She let herself go and pulled back just as quickly. For her I'd just been a momentary aberration.

My father, who's missed nothing of the scene asks me, with a roguish grin, 'I hope she gave you a nice blow-job at least.'

My mother shrugs her shoulders and drags us away from this den of iniquity. I hug my son and his smile, his kisses are balm to my wounded pride.

You leave your family in order to get away from your parents but above all from yourself. You want to leave your old self behind so that you can construct a different one. Know thyself: for the Greeks this imperative meant to be aware of your limitations. But we get to know ourselves quickly, we're not that unfamiliar with ourselves. How sad, when that is done, to be nothing but your own self and to be incapable of forgetting who you are. To go beyond yourself, to surprise yourself – that's the great art. Adolescence is the age of crossroads where we feel we're being bombarded by so many possible routes we're paralysed by their abundance. At the same time we're aware that the window of opportunity is narrow, the jaws of the vice will soon close, the slipknot will slowly tighten again, hardly allowing us to breathe. To grow up is to start by betraying, by crossing frontiers, breaking loose, leaving one's village that's too small, one's too-familiar language, one's too-tame kith and kin, to choose a nation, a culture in a new homeland. With a place at the Lycée Henri IV in Paris, I made feverish preparations for my departure, certain that a different, more densely packed life awaited me only a few hours away by train. My future was about to start, I was going to take my life in hand, get out of the sticky provincial mud, the monotonous Papa-Maman Hell. I wasn't disappointed: the capital surpassed all my expectations.

I arrived in Paris on a marvellous late afternoon in September that was bathed in exuberant light. Coming out of the *métro* at Saint-Germain-des-Prés, with one glance I found freedom, beauty and intelligence. The café terraces were crammed with elegant, sun-tanned men and women, devotees of the cult of pleasure and of conversation. Their relaxed bodies expressed the independence of mind, the easy-going mores that contrasted with the rigidity of the companions of my youth. It was that magical hour of conspiracies, of clandestine pacts made before nightfall, a concentration of ethnic groups, of skin colours, of languages, of appearances such as I'd never seen before. In an area not much bigger than a village square the most extravagant, most dissimilar beings were passing to and fro. I was ashamed of the way I looked, of my ignorance, of my close-cropped scalp. I looked like a country bumpkin. I couldn't take my eyes off these improbable creatures laughing out loud, smoking, kissing each other full on the lips.

In Paris I met Algerians, Africans, Vietnamese, Americans, Ashkenazim, Sephardim for the first time. I went towards them, drawn by their strangeness. I was astonished to discover how like me they were: we had the same aspirations, the same frustrations, the same desire to escape from the groups to which we belonged. I also discovered tribes with unknown names: communists, Trotskyists, feminists, Lambertists, situationists, Maoists, anarchists, anarcho-syndicalists, all at loggerheads with each other, settling their differences with iron bars and abuse. I immediately swung to the left, a rather libertarian left because everything was happening there, even though I've never belonged to any party. We would sing revolutionary songs such as '*Avanti Popolo*', '*Bella Ciao*', '*La Jeune Garde*' the better to free ourselves from nostalgia for the totalitarian past. The left-wing movements of 1968 were a trick of history that allowed communism to be eliminated among the intelligentsia by reviving its dogmas in the short term. I didn't want to miss out on what was going on at the time, to pass by what was best in it, its madness, its inventiveness, even its dead ends. I've never been a communist, a Trotskyite or a Maoist. For several years I roamed from one leftish sect to another as the mood took me, I even spent a few months in the PSU (Unified Socialist Party) and I remember Michel Rocard teaching us the rudiments of urban guerilla warfare on a beach in Corsica. I still have a good laugh about that. But right from the start I preferred the beatnik and hippie movements to the doctrinaire followers of Marxism-Leninism, I was more Charles Fourier than Lenin, more Allen Ginsberg than Antonio Gramsci, more Krishnamurti than Mao Tse-tung. Many years later I was to hear Allen Ginsberg recite his poem *Howl* in the City Lights Bookshop in San Francisco, a frenzied aesthetic manifesto, a sublime cry of rage against America and modern life: he grunted and groaned, ranted and raved, went into trances and the public left stunned by his performance. I was to come across him again in 1995 in Palo Alto; he was already ill, his head more hairless than ever with two portholes instead of eyes. I briefly told him how much I admired him.

I've never really left the progressive camp despite its thick-headed stupidity and moral self-satisfaction. When you reach my age you don't leave your adoptive family, you move away from it. Even today it's only the follies of the left that annoy me, the rest don't bother me at all. I prefer to remain a thorn in the flesh of my own camp, to undermine it from inside rather than desert it.

I fell in love with Paris, both its magical and its squalid sides. I was completely taken with it and have never shaken that feeling off. I'm not interested in dreaming my life away or living out my dreams: I've never suffered disenchantment because reality has always surpassed my expectations. The world bears greater riches than our poor hearts. In Paris – that my father loathed of course – I learnt that beauty is partly ugliness, pleasure partly pain, that opposites fraternise. The Seine is that revolting soup flowing between two banks, a septic tank with metallic glints and barges and river boats going up and down. I instantly wanted to be part of the left bank, of the bohemian youth, of the café-crème culture with its impassioned conversations. For me Paris has always been and still is the erotic city par excellence where a glance can set your senses blazing like a bundle of tinder. I gorged on incredible faces, seeing the public area as a breeding ground for all possible intrigues. I came to understand the goal of all existence: to blend truth and beauty. I began to expect to get everything from the streets: my substance, my poetry, my sensual pleasures. I lived out my life in small, smoky cafés, in those little mobile gatherings that keep the flow of participants moving and also filter it. You're never alone there, never too many, everyone's within sight and earshot, you group together according to affinity. The city was saying: everything's possible. It told me to stay on the alert, to keep away from the cloistered bliss of a couple. If there's any meaning to the word prayer, it must be the one I said to myself that evening: show yourself worthy of all this.

Chapter 5

The Great Awakeners

I'm twenty-one, I'm sitting in the sunshine, pen in hand, the window wide open onto Rue Guisarde, reading Hegel's *Phenomenology of Spirit* in the French translation by Jean Hippolyte. My son Eric, hardly a few months old, is wailing in his cradle. We're playing philosopher. I read out loud to him a few well-expressed sentences from the great German:

' "Each self-consciousness seeks the death of the other." Now what d'you think of that my little poppet?'

He babbles on without listening, chewing his rattle.

'I can see you're fascinated by that. Hey, look, here's something that concerns you personally: "The birth of the child is the death of the parents." D'you realise that means that our disappearance is structurally entailed in your arrival in the world. A bit discouraging, isn't it? For me at any rate.'

After I've read out ten sentences he falls asleep or starts to cry. Hegel isn't recommended for infants. The next day I'll read him a bit of Schopenhauer or Heidegger, some scraps of *Being and Time* to sharpen his mind and imbue it with wisdom. We're living with his mother, Violaine, an actress and primary school teacher, the daughter of a former fighter in the International Brigade who lost his leg on the Madrid front in 1937; it's a 17-square-metre flat in the Mabillon District, one room with cooking facilities and seatless toilets on the landing. It's 1970s France, sparing on soap and bathrooms. When, six months after he was born in 1970, my parents heard, with some excitement, of the existence of my son, all my father could think of to say was, 'Thank God her mother's not Jewish, Arab or African.'

The worst came first. They immediately became passionately attached to the child and wanted to take it over.

Violane and I are stony broke, in the evening she goes out into the streets to sing songs by Barbara, Jean Ferrat, Gilles Vigneault, some she's written herself; I go round with the hat, I feel I'm the luckiest of men. I listen to Léo Ferré over and over again: '*Avec le temps tout s'en va*' (With time everything goes), a song that's devastating in its strength and simplicity. At an age when, with time, everything comes, everything arrives, especially the best things, I gorge on hypothetical unhappiness. I've failed the *agrégation* in philosophy and the competitive examination for the *École Normale Superieure*[10] and I'm congratulating myself on that whilst my mother's tearing her hair out. We'd heard so many people telling us that exams were going to disappear that I botched the tests. Now I'm assessing my good fortune in having escaped the path my colleagues will follow. Whether as a graduate of the *École Normale Supérieure* or as an *agrégé*, I would have had to

10 *Agrégation* is the highest teaching qualification; the *École Normale Supérieure* is an elite institution, outside the university system but taking students up to doctoral and research level.

endure the indifference of mocking pupils, climb the rungs of the career ladder and conform in order to please my superiors. I have taught, but later on and under different conditions. What I've gained in freedom I've lost in security. It has sometimes cost me dear. I've remained an eternal student, pen in hand, filling notebooks with clumsy drawings, picking up the classics as if I were opening them for the first time. As I get older I assess the increasing extent of my ignorance which, far from depressing me, makes me look forward to dazzling new discoveries.

I had to make my own way, take a leap into the unknown with the anxiety that entails. I decided, in a gamble lacking any basis in reason, to live by my pen. I survived mostly on grants, little jobs: night-watchman, working freelance for girlie magazines, usher, literacy teacher in a company (they would call me 'Mr Wog' when I arrived on the premises at the end of the working day – most of those who attended the course in the basement came from North Africa), grape-picker, restaurant waiter, bar pianist – I would happily murder standards in noisy rooms, with much waving of the hands, thunderous blues, interminable improvisations. The worst happened when a professional offered to accompany me, ending up, after a few chords, outshining me, relegating my performance to the level of laboured sound effects. At twenty-six I happened by chance to get a position as a copywriter for an insurance company. As I was going to the office on the first morning I noticed my reflection in a shop window and was horrified by what I saw: a young pen-pusher, briefcase in hand, about to be caught up in the *métro-boulot-dodo* (tube-work-sleep) spiral, as they called the daily grind in those days. I immediately turned tail. I'd rather tighten my belt than demean myself. For years, to the despair of my parents, who daily predicted a catastrophe,

I lived in a state of happy precariousness, indulging in the supreme luxury: the life of the mind and free time. Throughout my childhood I had heard my father, whose dream was to see me as a government official, boring me with his creed of submissiveness: 'Don't make a fuss, keep a low profile, be at meetings ahead of time, agree with the opinions of your superiors and remember that the future belongs to those who get up early.'

It's hardly surprising then that I've made liberal use of provocation in my books, detested constraints and for a long time preferred the night-time world. I got my sustenance from clear Chinese or Vietnamese soups with powerful aromas and unbeatable prices. The public health authorities kept closing them down one after the other for the illegal use of rats, dogs and cats in their food, but we still tucked in all the same. Those little creatures are better than their reputation. I was doing the work I'd chosen, I had the greatest works of world culture at my disposal, I wasn't subject to set hours. I was part of an aristocracy of studious leisure: I had little money but I spent every winter in Asia, living for three months on an amount I would have squandered in a fortnight in Paris. In January I would go from Goa to Yogykarta and Ko Samui, from Penang to Rangoon, ending up in Ibiza in August. I immediately made India my adoptive country, as aghast at the poverty as carried away by the splendour, the elegance, the refinement of that nation, the womb of all Asiatic civilisations.

I set off for those countries assured I wouldn't come across any trace of my own, even indirectly, unlike in Africa or the Mahgreb. I went there fatigued with my own culture and in order to recharge my batteries, seeking an alternate world that would redeem me. I arrived in Bombay at the moment when the former hippies, those tatterdemalion princes, were metamorphosing into beggars, dying by the roadside from dysentery, exhaustion, overdoses, to the indifference of the locals. I savoured the pleasure of disappearing in the crowd, of being an unknown person amid millions of anonymous ones, carried along by the stream of bodies in movement. To pay for my travels I managed to place occasional long articles in serious journals, pieces on the politics of New Delhi, the tensions between religions on the subcontinent, the situation of the sacred cow (I feel affection for those animals and their lovely moist eyes) or the re-Islamisation of the Malay region. I was enthusiastic, carefree, confident my luck would hold. For me writing has always been inseparable from a way of life: style above all things, an aesthetic quality of existence, the enjoyment of little things, the hope of big ones. Not to give up anything, neither philosophy nor the novel, nor children's stories, nor drama: that was my gamble from the days of my adolescence, a gamble on loyalty to a certain French tradition. I've been lucky, I have to admit, my books worked at once, times were easier than they are today.

Books have saved me. From despair, from stupidity, from cowardice, from boredom. The great works lift us up above ourselves, broaden our minds so that we fit into a spiritual republic. To enter that is like setting out on the high seas or taking apart an extremely sophisticated clockwork mechanism. I had already made a start on several mighty peaks of philosophy and I'd had the impression I could breathe more easily in their company. The fascinating thing about systems of thought is that they give substance to the absurd little ideas that come to us all some time or other: why is there something rather than nothing, are we alone in the world, what can we legitimately hope for? I love the sensual aspect of philosophy and I love philosophy as a sensualist. I cannot conceive of the exchange of ideas without a poetic and carnal dimension. Asking questions with no answer, answering questions that haven't been asked, that seems to me to constitute the enigmatic greatness of that discipline even if it is too often corrupted by the spirit of seriousness that makes things look obscure in order to look profound. How often have I mixed with professionals in the concept business who can't butter a slice of bread without quoting Nietzsche or Spinoza, with those devotees of wisdom who, worn down by work, reach retirement in bitterness, having taken a dislike to their students and dreaming too late of a more far-reaching destiny? They thought they were at the summit of universal intelligence and life has passed them by. With them the Spirit bloweth not. They can talk about anything but don't know what they're talking about. Books have fed them, books have killed them. The marvellous occupation of professor dies through repetition of the same ideas if it's not permanently inspired by a sort of missionary vibration, if it's not the art of winning over minds, of lifting up hearts. I admire the great scholars, the adventurers of the spirit. But even more I like the unfrocked thinkers who can develop a brilliant argument and at the same time can enjoy the good things in life, make fun of themselves, laugh at the comedy society presents. Woe betide anyone who takes himself for a sovereign pope, strikes the pose of a magus or a prophet. He's in danger of being revealed as a sham. St Francis of Assisi saw himself as the juggler of God. More modestly, intellectuals are the jesters of middle-class society, nothing more, nothing less. The middle classes are wiser than them when they put them in their place.

I've never finished *The Phenomenology of Spirit* nor *Time and Being,* I left them hanging in the air half way through but I know their dénouements. A happy ending in one case, tragic in the other. I'll go back to them one day, but with caution: I have an intuition that certain books should not be finished as that might entail the disappearance of the reader. Pure superstition, I agree. I have a special relationship with certain masterpieces mired in their own perfection that I want to get read so that I don't have to go back to them any more. I start them, I get a taste of them, I put them aside regretfully, I pick them up again wearily. Even if I've finished them I have the feeling I've not understood them and ought to start from the beginning again. They require a psychological investment that ought to be balanced out with some reward. I've opened most of the major novels of world literature without having dared to go through them from beginning to end for fear of annihilating myself.

Thus in the summer of 2012 I decided, while visiting the American West, to take up Thomas Mann's *The Magic Mountain* and read it right through, from beginning to end. My main interest in it was because the story takes place in a sanatorium for people with tuberculosis, the Berghof in Davos, Switzerland, before the First World War. It relates the dramatic adventures of Hans Castorp, who has come from Hamburg to spend a few weeks with his cousin Joachim. As he discovers the strange society of patients, whose main occupation consists in trying to decipher the X-rays of their lungs, he contracts the disease, falls in love with a young Russian woman, Claudia Chauchat, a passion that will never be consummated, and stays there for seven years, high in the mountains, until the declaration of war in 1914 when he leaves to fight in the trenches. It seems to me that one of the things Thomas Mann is trying to do is to turn the perspectives upside down: the society of the patients, although distorted in appearance, is more civilised than that of the world of the 'flatlands', that is about to tumble into the barbarity of the War. Healthy people are sick but unaware of it, while the so-called sick possess minds of greater lucidity. Bourgeois culture, refined as it is, is going to bring about events of unimaginable barbarity. I'd started the book thirty years before. For the first 400 pages I was dazzled, wearied for the following 300, exhausted by the last. I cheated, skipped the didactic passages, the long dissertations and reached the end completely out of breath. In his preface Thomas Mann refuted in advance the claim that it was boring by asking readers to take their time to read the story and to put themselves in the place of one of the characters. A book that was written over several years demands to be read over a lengthy period. My father, convinced that Thomas Mann was a Jew, condemned the writer for the worst of reasons: his fierce opposition to Hitler. It so happened that he died the day after I finished that huge tome. No question of cause and effect, I agree, but I saw it as a sign.

The only way of escaping from your family is to find others, to tie yourself in spirit to new traditions. Hardly had I arrived in Paris than my curiosity focused on all the leading figures of the literary world. One incident alone will suffice to show my relations with my substitute fathers. A novice has blind faith in the older people he admires. My first master was my philosophy teacher in the first year of the preparatory course for the *École Normale Supérieure* examination, M. Bloch. He could talk without notes on Kant, Rousseau, Hegel, and I took it all down in exercise books with margins that I still have today. He was brilliant, both clear and profound, the two necessary qualities for a teacher. He was one of those whose teaching is uplifting and can determine your vocation in the course of one class. He had a flair for dialectical reversal that left us flabbergasted – us, the little provincials who had come to the capital to sharpen up both mind and body. His classes were a delight and I would have liked to learn them off by heart even as he was giving them. In the parallel class René Schérer held sway. A specialist on Husserl with the profile of a bird of prey who had taken from Charles Fourier the idea of erotic hospitality for young children, he, along with Guy Hocquenghem, was an advocate of pederasty. One day M. Bloch took me to his house, near Val-de-Grâce, to give me back a piece of work he'd marked. We had hardly opened the door when an extremely shrill voice shouted from the living-room, 'Slippers, Raymond!'

My philosophical idol gave me an apologetic look, shrugged his shoulders and pointed to a heap of dirty pieces of felt on the doormat. We slithered in, wobbling on these slippers, and at the same time my enthusiasm began to wobble as well. His wife, a frail little lady but with substantial vocal timbre, checked our feet then ran off to shut herself away in her room. I left, my exercise in my hand, unable to stick the pieces of my shattered ideal back together again. I felt that such a brilliant man could only live in a sublime apartment with a remarkable woman at his side. That was the day when I decided never to be a teacher, to avoid that career if the cost was such a compromise. In retrospect my attitude seems so uncompromising as to be stupid. A great teacher, in his personal life M. Bloch was a good husband, anxious to preserve domestic peace. That he had to swap his shoes for a pair of felt slippers seems to me a hygienic measure: after all, many cultures require one to take one's shoes off before crossing the threshold of a house so as not to bring in foul matter from outside. But youth is a foolish age, the age of the absolute that hasn't yet learnt the art of the nuance.

It's one thing to take on masters, another, and more agonising, to see them get into difficulties or go into decline. In 1967 I witnessed an uproar round Jean-Paul Sartre at the *École Normale Supérieure* in Rue d'Ulm. He'd come to talk about existentialism but his time was over. Newcomers were challenging him from the left, a generation of young professors – Althusser, Derrida, Deleuze, Foucault – who declared themselves antihumanists. Like the character Chick in Boris Vian's novel *L'Écume des jours*, I was addicted to 'Jean-Sol Partre',[11] an abstruse and pretentious preacher who stirs up crowds and can say almost anything, sure of arousing enthusiasm and unanimous agreement. Sartre was my hero, the man I'd revered from my earliest youth, the man who'd taught me the necessity of revolt and the twists and turns of bad faith, whose mores, whose intellectual gunfire had been electrifying France for thirty years, who'd taught us, amongst other splendid things, 'to make something out of what others have made of us.' My father hated him, wanted to have him shot because of his support for the FLN[12] during the Algerian war. That made me cherish him even more.

That afternoon at the *École Normale Supérieure* he wasn't at his best. His opaque right eye was eating up his face. Hardly had he opened his mouth than ten or so dandies in the front row started to exclaim out loud, 'Oh, what anguissshe, what anguissshe!' referring to what he says in *La Nausée* (*Nausea*) about the viscosity of being and man's panic at being thrown into the world for no apparent reason. Sartre pretended not to hear them and continued his presentation in a toneless voice,

---

11 The name of the character in the novel is a spoonerism on Jean-Paul Sartre. *L'Écume des jours* has been variously translated as *Froth on the Daydream, Foam of the Daze* and *Mood Indigo.*

12 The Algerian National Liberation Front in the war against France.

only getting meagre applause. For the time being he was out of fashion while he outshone – and that by a lot – all the candidates for the succession. I was scandalised at the lack of respect shown to my idol, I had witnessed an act of sacrilege. I saw him again one year later at the Sorbonne, at the beginning of May '68. He was tiny beside Claude Lanzmann and Simone de Beauvoir, lost in the middle of a crowd of large and exceedingly hirsute guys. He had difficulty making himself heard, he wanted to 'put himself at the service of the masses and the revolution,' he wanted to be where he could listen to the younger generation. He was constantly interrupted by cries of, 'Shut your trap, Sartre.' The anti-authoritarian rebellion was in full swing, everyone used the familiar 'tu' to each other, a Nobel prizewinner knew no more than someone who'd just passed their *baccalauréat*. You could sense the pleasure of the juvenile crowd in taking a sacred monster down a peg or two, in dragging him down to their own level.

I was saddened by this, just as it offended me a few years later to see him perched on a barrel to speak to the Renault workers at Île Billancourt or selling *La Cause du peuple,* an extreme left-wing rag, on street corners, always looking for the magic of a liaison between the proletariat and the intellectuals. It also upset me to see him harnessed by the fanatical Maoists of the *Gauche Prolétarienne* (Proletarian Left) and their leader Pierre Victor, alias Benny Lévy, a charismatic and authoritarian personality of varying dogma who loved to be the incarnation of the super-ego in all discussions with a third party. According to Simone de Beauvoir, what they were doing with him amounted to the veritable corruption of an old man. It is true, as he explained in an interview with François Samuelson, that with them he found a certain kind of friendship, of communion he'd never experienced with the communists. For him it was a way of growing old in the limelight.

I was in the lounge of Calcutta Airport when I heard of his death. I had just arrived from Sikkim and Darjeeling, and it affected me as if a piece of my youth had sunk into oblivion. By then I had grown away from him politically: I had been annoyed by his extended flirtation with Stalinism and Castroism (the theoretician of absolute freedom becoming the eulogist of total servitude), his solidarity with the Communist Party, his call for colonists to be put to death in his preface to Frantz Fanon's *Damnés de la terre* (*The Wretched of the Earth*), his quarrel with Camus and Aron, who were both so much more clear-sighted than him in the face of the phenomenon of totalitarianism. And I made a vehement attack on him in *Le Sanglot de l'homme blanc* (*The Tears of the White Man*).

But today, and in spite of his political aberrations, I can find in the early Sartre material to refute the Sartre of his mature years. I continue to salute him as a kind of effervescent genius, a magic polygraph, at least in his early works. His failures are as instructive as his commitments and throughout his long and stirring life there were no limits to the generosity he showed: he gave unstinting – and sometimes unthinking – support to a wide variety of causes as well as handing out unhesitatingly considerable sums from his own pocket to anyone who asked. In comparison with the minor masters who followed him in the '70s and '80s, he remains incontestably a giant, if a much-debated giant.

From these incidents I take a simple lesson: there's no such thing as a supreme thinker. A great artist can be fallible, exasperating, and still continue to fascinate us. We love him with all his contradictions, astounded by his good qualities, sorry for his erring ways. As a general rule it's better not to meet authors one venerates for fear of being disillusioned.

Confining ourselves to the classics saves us from the double burden of envy and disappointment, while a contemporary, however great he might be, is also an ordinary man who pays his taxes, utters banalities, catches colds. There's a cruel element in admiration because it cannot pardon any shortcoming. It's a swift journey from adulation to dismissal when our chosen object no longer matches up to our expectations. That's the danger of going to see the Great Writer. I experienced this on the occasion of a conversation with Albert Cohen. Together with a friend, Maurice Partouche, I'd gone to Geneva to interview him for *Le Monde* in 1980. I expected a personality at least as flamboyant as his Solal and I'd just finished his *Belle du Seigneur* on the night train and been very impressed with it. We were greeted by an old man in a silk dressing gown, delightfully urbane but very conventional in what he said. He was unwaveringly misogynistic and confined his wife to the role of cook and substitute mother. Lunch was an insipid *brandade* of cod, probably out of a tin. Even the furnishings of his apartment were very plain while I was expecting a sort of Oriental palace. The disenchantment was immediate. Since then I've never opened a book of his again, nor eaten *brandade* of cod, even though every year I promise myself I'll make good that double injustice.

All only sons seek a brother in spirit with whom they can share things they can't tell their parents. In my case it was Alain Finkielkraut. We'd known each other since I had gone to Henri IV but our real meeting was in Dublin during a language course at Trinity College in the year of the release of The Beatles' *Sergeant Pepper's Lonely Hearts Club Band,* that we adored. We dissected it song by song with the meticulousness of Talmudists, looking for poetic correspondences, the subliminal message behind the words. Spontaneously and in all modesty we shared out the roles, he was Paul McCartney, I was John Lennon. It was a strange summer I spent there: I was going out with a hotheaded Irish girl – Ireland, it's the baroque, Catholic madness exacerbated by the hatred of England – who could think of nothing better for the night before I went back to France than to stab me with a knife below my shoulder blade to punish me for leaving. The blade only scratched me and tore my jacket but I was deeply moved by her aggression and took her there, in the driving rain on the slope of a canal, by way of farewell.

A long time afterwards, Alain and I found we were neighbours in the Odéon District of Paris. This geographical coincidence brought us together. We would run into each other morning, noon and night and gradually became inseparable. One day, exasperated by the same thunderous speeches about sexual liberation – he and I were both allergic to the dominant discourse – we decided to get together to let the other side of the story be heard. I had by then, after five years of having my manuscripts rejected by different publishers, published one essay and one novel. I had sent out samples to anyone and everyone, including Simone de Beauvoir and Claude Roy – all had replied, given me support and comfort. I can appreciate their generosity today when I myself am approached by young writers. Alain and I decided to put our intuitions together, each of us writing a chapter after discussion with the other. It was the easiest, most spontaneous writing ever undertaken. Each supplied nuance and lucidity to the other, we created a third person made up of the qualities of the first two. As a pair we were stronger, quicker, more intelligent. Young, we were just two first names engaged in precise projects; our family names, origins, religion hardly existed any more.

When, in 1978–9, I went to visit Alain for a few months in

Berkeley, where he was guest professor, the counter-culture movement was running out of steam: the former heroes of the rebellion were finishing up as tramps or businessmen. We had chosen '*Our House*', a song by Crosby, Stills, Nash & Young celebrating home, cats and flowers, as our anthem of friendship. The evening I arrived in San Francisco, Christmas Eve, Alain and his girlfriend Sabine took me to the Castro district, the centre of the burgeoning gay community: in a dark street with potholed pavements two solidly built guys were making savage love. I watched them, dumbfounded. And slightly jealous: why didn't heterosexuals behave so openly? That reminds me of something Foucault said one day when we were expounding our different conceptions of love: Alain was more sentimental, I more flighty. Foucault brushed us aside with a mocking smile: 'There's one thing I've never understood and that's the meaning of the expression 'Don Juanism'. I can sleep with ten different partners in a single night, so I don't see what's exceptional about a man who keeps a meticulous list of his conquests.'

Alain and I used to have unresolvable metaphysical debates: was it or was it not necessary to make oneself look older in order to appear more serious, thus escaping from the indecisiveness of youth? He quoted the passage from *The World of Yesterday* where Stefan Zweig tells how from the age of ten he forced himself to wear starched collars so as to appear grown up. He always had a fund of brilliant quotations to hand that illuminated our conversations, never allowing himself to think other than in the wake of great forerunners, a characteristic I've taken from him. Should you have a book under your arm when walking down the street or going on a date? I was in favour of empty hands. It was a matter of style, one shouldn't smell of sweat. I wanted to lighten my load, he to cram himself full of knowledge. Even today I keep my reading hidden in a pocket, covered by a newspaper, so I don't look as if I'm 'putting it on', while he's often lugging heavy satchels.

Alain had helped me avoid military service thanks to a subtle stratagem set up with a psychiatrist friend. He had just been declared unfit for service by the same means. After spending a week smoking heavily, not eating anything, not sleeping much, I went one evening, in a very poor state, to the A&E department of a hospital in the northern suburbs, claiming I'd tried to commit suicide with barbiturates. In fact I'd only swallowed one and a half Valium tablets. The point was to be groggy while remaining conscious, in case the physicians should try to pump my stomach and discover the trick. It worked. I was taken into hospital and spent three days in a psychiatric ward with patients who had genuine mental illnesses, who would stop by my bed for an hour, stand with their faces stuck to the wall, hum, shout abuse. The nurses, convinced there was a disappointment in love behind my attempt, took it in turns to sit by my bed and console me. I was cared for, pampered and cosseted. A military doctor summoned me to Vincennes, to the recruitment centre. He examined my file and subjected me to a prolonged interrogation. I spoke about my suicidal tendencies, my inability to accept my role as a father. Eventually the colonel said, 'I'm sure you're simulating but I've no way of proving it. As there is some doubt, I prefer to release you from your obligation to do military service.'

I was so delighted with this that I locked myself in the lavatory, overcome with an irrepressible fit of laughter. After my faked suicide attempt (SI) I was declared P4 (psychiatric 4), a classification that in principle closed the doors for me to any post in the public service.[13] I couldn't have cared less. I had escaped a year of barrack-life and latrine duty. Despite the respect I feel for the army and my admiration for its achievements, I am very pleased that I managed to shirk that obligation.

Alain had the laugh of an urchin who's been caught out and was perpetually juggling with a pencil in his left hand to help him think. You would be distracted by the movement while he developed his arguments. He was astonished at everything, improvised feverishly, was able to sum up a situation in a word with a remarkable turn of phrase, while retaining his winning smile. Sometimes we went with my son to have lunch with his parents, who were welcoming and cordial. Forty years on I can still remember their address and telephone number in the 10th arrondissement, close to the Gare de l'Est. As the years passed, Alain and I developed the characteristics of twins: our similarity in physique, voice and dress became so close that we were frequently mistaken for each other. We shared certain girlfriends who had no intention of going out with the one without trying the other. When we wrote to each other, our sentences were constructed on the same model, we had a taste for unusual words, inverted aphorisms, roundabout ways of putting things, schoolboy jokes. We eventually came to resemble each other to the point where we were each disappearing in the other, where we no longer knew what was our own self. We had become duplicates, Siamese twins, too close to be a duo, too distinct to be just one. It went so far that we each envied the other his illnesses that marked him

13 In France this takes in a much wider group than just the civil service and includes other 'employees of the state' such as teachers and those working in social security, the post office and French Railways.

out. Our relationship would then be in danger of descending into confrontation through an excess of symbiosis. Rivalry is the most widely spread feeling in the intellectual milieu; it encourages an element of healthy emulation but can always descend into sterile jealousy. In that case one has to change one's rival, one's model, that is. In love as in friendship, passion and duration rarely make good partners; it is better to have solid and temperate affections that keep going through time, rather than a brief flare of passion with no tomorrow.

Thus it was that our intimacy made strangers of us and it was an irremediable estrangement that no later familiarity could dissipate. We decided to go our separate ways in order to preserve our respective identities, to draw a demarcation line between us. The separation lasted almost ten years. It wasn't disagreement that set us apart but imitation. It was a painful but necessary amputation. Even today, when we hardly ever see each other any more, I feel I'm listening to myself when he takes part in a discussion on the radio and I finish some of his sentences in my mind before he does. We react in a similar way to certain events, as if we were in telepathic communication. Our own books echo each other, responding, borrowing, contradicting. We have each set up exclusive reserves on which we are both constantly trespassing, such is our desire to encroach on the other's territory. We have never lost sight of each other, even our calumnies are just a further way of getting news of the other person.

Despite all this we have, with time, like twins who end up being different from each other, managed to develop a difference and a major one at that: Alain is deeply pessimistic about the future of the human race while I, conversely, believe in the power of freedom to surmount the problems that face it. He seems to despair of mankind, while I never cease to marvel at it. He is full of nostalgia for the past, while my appetites are entirely directed towards the present. Where he sees catastrophes, I perceive transformations. He hates technology, is very unhappy about the Internet, while I take advantage of it as far as is possible with my limited competence. He sometimes seems so unhappy, so moving, lost in unfathomable depths of anguish, that one feels like comforting him, telling him the world will survive us and has no need of us. After all, we're nothing but acrobats in the circus of ideas. If the ship should founder, it's better to drink a cheery toast to the shipwreck rather than go down lamenting. At least there are things we've kept in common: our passion for controversy, our devotion to books, our hatred of fanaticism and indifference to honours. Beyond the quarrels and sensitivities he is and will ever remain my brother in ink.

Around 1973 I started a doctoral thesis on the utopian pre-Marxist Charles Fourier with Roland Barthes. I had written to him suggesting a subject and he had agreed immediately. Barthes was a simple man, easy to get on with, generous with his time and his thought. He had a warm, beautifully resonant voice, an intelligence that he used without crushing other people. His seminars gave rise to innumerable ardent declarations from bold and beautiful young men. He would cut them short, not wanting to turn his classes into a cruising zone. Each one of his books was an event that we discussed passionately. His famous remark in 1972: 'Suddenly I couldn't care less about not being modern,' had been a welcome bolt from the blue to our ears, releasing us from a suffocating straitjacket. If he, the icon of hyper-modernity, could allow himself such freedom, it meant that an epoch was coming to an end, that a gap was opening up in the packed defence of theory we had been subjected to for so long. Finally we had the right to read the great novels without disdain or a guilty conscience. It wasn't just Marxism that was breaking down but also the intellectual terrorism of the avant-gardes and their daring but now stale innovations. In those days we were pompous, prattling fools, dandies that were pathetic though full of good will. Barthes never went anywhere without his entourage of faithful retainers who looked askance at any newcomer and tried to shoo him away, like fly-swatting slaves protecting their sovereign from the buzz of insects. It was strange: everyone in his seminar spoke as he did, reproducing his mannerisms, his neologisms, catching his tics as if by a sort of spontaneous contagion. Around him this professor, with his love of the multitude of languages, only heard one idiom, his own, spread by all his pupils transformed into learned parrots.

I took the viva for my doctorate with him one morning in May 1975 in a room in the University of Jussieu, a hideous concrete block defacing the banks of the Seine. Only my friend Laurent Aublin was there to hear me defend my thesis and I regretted not having rounded up more support. My mother had begged to be allowed to come to witness the ceremony but I had gone down on my knees to dissuade her and, just to be safe, had lied about the date and place in order to avoid the comic situation of an advocate of libertinism with his mummy holding his hand. She would have been capable of getting up without warning and saying in a loud voice what she would often tell me, 'You know, my son has never got over having something inside his trousers.'

My examiners also included Gérard Genette and Julia Kristeva, both of them dry pedants who adopted from the start the attitude of Marxists mandarins, which is what they were at the time. As was his wont, Barthes was both perspicacious and kindly-disposed. The slightly provocative title of my thesis was: *The body of each of us belongs to everyone*. In it I was proposing a kind of libidinal communism developed from the Fourierist theory of the amorous exchange. Barthes commented that there was a coercive, almost inhuman aspect to such a utopia if it was to be translated into reality, it was more closely related to de Sade's republican ideal than to Fourier's phalanstery. Barthes was suggesting the alternative interpretation rather than insisting on it, putting forward his argument without humiliating me. Unlike his two fellow examiners, who were proud of displaying their learning, he was careful not to make a show of the phallic power of the master; he knew how to keep a low profile and allow his pupil to find the way towards the truth himself. My thesis was accepted and I was relieved. In my hand I had a diploma that was prestigious and of no value on the labour market, I was the very example of the impoverished student so common nowadays, heading for the educated proletariat. I could count on no one but myself. That was my good fortune.

Two years later Alain Finkielkraut and I were to publish, with du Seuil, *Le Nouveau Désordre amoureux* (*The New Love Disorder*). We were astonished to learn from our editor, Denis Roche, the man who had helped me to get my foot on the ladder by publishing my first essay on Charles Fourier, that Roland Barthes was asking, through François Wahl, for the publication of our essay to be deferred. He was about to bring out his own *Fragments d'un discours amoureux* (*A Lover's Discourse: Fragments*) and didn't want any competition, afraid that another book on the same theme might reduce the impact of his own. The reappearance of love in theoretical studies was beginning with dissension! Despite his preciosity and his affectations, that haven't aged very well, we loved Barthes: he had liberated us from a certain narrow-minded dogmatism and taught us to read the classics again. Too much under the influence of his friends at *Tel Quel*[14] he had made some comments unworthy of him on his voyage to Maoist China in 1974 (I can still recall his embarrassment in the seminar when we asked him, 'So what about Peking, the legacy of Mao?' and that he had veered off into a digression in praise of blandness) just as later on Michel Foucault got it wrong about the Iranian Revolution. But we were flabbergasted that a famous professor, who had recently been appointed to the Collège de France, should be concerned about the manuscript of two novices who admired him more than anyone else. However, we agreed to his conditions and the publication of *Nouveau Désordre amoureux* was put back six months, which did no harm whatsoever to the reception of the book that was an instant success, with pirated editions appearing throughout northern and eastern Europe. We were the first to emphasise, contrary to the 'unfettered enjoyment' of the situationists, that the emancipation of morals opened up new areas of intimacy to the market, establishing ruthless competition between individuals in erotic matters. We didn't hold our former mentor's action against him, we were too ambitious to be nothing but disciples, but I did stop seeing him. We didn't yet know that with every publication an author, whatever his age or position, longs to be recognised as he was when he'd just appeared on the scene and anxiously awaits the critics' judgment on his work. Every artist or writer, however famous he might be, has an obsessive fear that his voice will no longer be heard. You can never be cured of it, whatever people say, and to publish a book is to stake one's all once again, to submit oneself to the judgment of an invisible tribunal.

As I remember him, Barthes was a melancholy sensualist

14 An avant-garde literary review, published 1960–1982.

with an air of gravity scarcely concealed by his praise of the great sinners. Unlike Michel Foucault, who was openly bawdy and Rabelaisian, in many ways he had the sense of modesty of a young maiden and detested smutty talk. And contrary to Foucault, who was known for his bitchiness,[15] he never spoke ill of anyone, preferring to say nothing and remain silent if there was someone he didn't like. He intimidated me and when we had a drink together, I would rack my brains to keep the conversation going, afraid of boring him. Well aware that I didn't share his sexual proclivities, he would eye all the boys who walked past giving each of them winning smiles. One day, well before my thesis was accepted, I sent him a letter telling him what stage my work had reached and concluding with a little personal touch, an unhappy love affair that was upsetting me. He replied with a note containing the simple sentence, 'I'm sorry to hear you are unhappy' and that had touched me. I ran into him again on the Boulevard Saint-Germain a few months before his accident. He was an old, bowed man whose hair had gone white following his mother's death. We exchanged a few embarrassed words, I briefly offered him my condolences and we went our separate ways. I regret not having invited him for a drink. I ought to have given him my hand, told him how much he had meant to me and to thousands of others. Some remaining resentment, fear of appearing ridiculous? I let him go with the arrogance of youth towards age. Not being able to get over the death of his mother when he was over sixty seemed to me to be taking sensitivity to the extreme. I'm still annoyed with myself at this missed opportunity. Just as when you're fifteen you read novelists that are beyond you and never open them again, between eighteen and thirty with your couldn't-

15 To Jean Baudrillard, who in 1977 had published *Forget Foucault*, he retorted, 'My own problem is rather remembering who Baudrillard is.'

care-less attitude you fail to appreciate the exceptional people life puts in your way and whose true stature you only become aware of later. To understand them, to be able to put ourselves in their place, we have to be as old as they were when we met them. But by then it's too late.

Barthes was knocked down by a van in the Rue des Écoles in February 1980, as he was coming out of *Brasserie Bazar* after lunch with François Mitterrand, who at the time was a candidate for the presidency and of whom, moreover, he had a very low opinion. It's always dangerous for an intellectual to rub shoulders with those in power, even if it's only over a meal. There is a story doing the rounds that at the time Barthes had an American student's thesis on the representations of death in contemporary culture under his arm. The student, a former marine, summoned to defend his thesis, had landed in Paris on the very day his supervisor got run over. He had to return home and was, it appears, forever marked by the incident, as if by a curse. Barthes spent three weeks dying in hospital. With Michel Foucault we decided to organise a farewell ceremony when the funeral set off from the Paris morgue, the Institut Médico-Légal on the Quai de la Rapée. There were only a few of us, ten or so, on a grey, late-March morning, and my memory of it is one of infinite sadness. A life of such fame and such a solitary death!

A post-war paradox: the generation that put an end to paternal authority desperately went searching for substitute fathers. They hadn't rebelled to become free but to give themselves a new guardian. Some prostrated themselves before Mao, Castro or Che Guevara, others before some acknowledged intelligentsia guru, but the essential part was the prostrating. These fathers in spirit are equally capable of mystification, especially when they pose as heretics, calling for the masters to be trampled underfoot, the better to rule themselves. But their mistakes involve thousands, if not millions of followers and tragedies. Losing one's illusions is part, but not the whole of intellectual maturity. Beyond idolatry and disenchantment there remains our gratitude to the great awakeners. Watching an intellect emerge and spread its wings is a rare privilege for us. To all those who have passed on to us something of their clear-sightedness, have expanded our minds, we owe a big thank-you, eternal gratitude.

Part Three

In Final Settlement

Chapter 6

An Unforeseen Legacy

A terrible poem by Philip Larkin (1922–1985) famous in his own country as a misanthropist and misogynist:

> They fuck you up, your mum and dad.
>   They may not mean to, but they do.
> They fill you with the faults they had
>   And add some extra, just for you.
>
> But they were fucked up in their turn
>   By fools in old-style hats and coats,
> Who half the time were soppy-stern
>   And half at one another's throats.
>
> Man hands on misery to man.
>   It deepens like a coastal shelf.
> Get out as early as you can,
>   And don't have any kids yourself.[16]

16 *Collected Poems,* Farrar Straus and Giroux, 2001.

Rebelling gets you nowhere. The great thing is not to repeat the mistakes of the people you're rejecting. To challenge them is simply to pass them on unintentionally. What is true of family life applies equally to political life: every revolution deposes a dictator only to install another, yesterday's victim who, hardly has he assumed power than he sets about persecuting others himself. You don't go from servitude to freedom, you just change fetters. This was the vicious circle of the twentieth century, the tragedy of communism and its avatars. Faced with his father, a son has only three options: submission, escape or disobedience. These three can be mixed. Rebellion is often merely emulation speeded up: after having kicked over the traces, the child returns to follow in his father's wake. Believing he's making his getaway, he perpetuates the neurosis without realising or becomes a scapegoat, atoning for the sins of the others. For years I kept finding myself flying into rages strictly modelled on my father's, hysterical fits in which I start to bawl and shout, sucked ever deeper into a vortex of fury. It's a kind of trance: in my voice I can hear his voice bawling along with me. He's screaming in my throat, taking possession of my vocal chords. Like him, I go to extremes, turn into a demoniac stamping his feet. Despite myself I repeat exactly the same expressions my father used to my mother to the different women I have lived with. When I lose my temper like that, I hurry over to a mirror and I think that behind my contorted features I can see, in a kind of double exposure, his face giving me his orders. When I feel low, I tell myself that my life has been nothing but one long domestic row with different persons. The only people you can torture properly are those who love you. One day, in a moment of lucidity, he declared, 'You can detest me as much as you like, my revenge is that you're like me.'

Every father carries his children on his shoulders when they're small. And they, once they're grown up, carry their father, as did Aeneas when he carried Anchises on his back out of the ruins of Troy; on their shoulders, on the back of their necks they feel the weight of an invasive creature that has amalgamated with them and is devouring them like an incubus or a *dybbuk* in the cabbalistic tradition. Even the weakest of progenitors manage to impose their prejudices, their manias. What a terrible disappointment: to believe yourself free and discover you're preconditioned. Our acts are determined in advance, all spontaneity is the family lie coming out through us. Everyone is caught up in their genealogy, like a fly in a spider's web, trying to keep their heads up, to get their footing.

There's nothing more difficult than being a father, he crushes his children whatever he is: as a celebrity with his fame, as a swine with his loathsomeness, as an ordinary man with his mediocrity. He can also be a mediocre celebrity, a touching swine. Whatever he does, he's wrong: either it's too much or not enough. One day he's suffocating his offspring, another his sin is his absence – all the men of my generation have been intermittent fathers. And when he shows affection, it leads to ironic comments about how his feminine side's coming out, how he's going soft. I always find it moving to see young fathers playing with their children in the park, changing their nappies, feeding them, telling them stories, covering them with kisses. The contemporary family is an emotional union: everything from bibs to pocket money is negotiable, everything is smoothed out in outpourings of sentiment. We bring up our children so that one day they can leave us, and they do so when we need them more than they need us. It makes the separation even more of a wrench. A world without fathers doesn't seem a very desirable place, the proof lying in the single-parent families: there are no good mothers any more once there are only mothers. What takes the place of the father is the society of brothers that leads to the dictatorship of the little gangs with an absolute disciplinary structure. Then the sole rite of passage becomes the riot, the confrontation with the police or with other gangs. Our police and the CRS[17] would be amazed if we told them that, with their helmets, boots and truncheons, they were helping the young men who insult them to grow up. Nowadays going to demonstrations, being beaten up and taken in for questioning constitute the psychological school-leaving exam of our adolescents. It's an expensive, sometimes bloody but indispensable ritual.

So my father will have passed on to me his aggressiveness, a detestable characteristic in everyday life but a cardinal virtue for an intellectual whose business it is, amongst other things, to stir up controversies. My mother, for her part, liked to think she'd infected me with her fitful sleep. Whenever I woke up tired, moaning that I hadn't slept a wink, she would pat me on the head and say, affectionately, 'You get that from me.'

With age insomnia has become a way of life. It's a total experience, with no prospect of respite, piling two states on top of each other: panic and resurrection. In the small hours the night looms over you like a verdict with no appeal. The least concern takes on immeasurable proportions, you feel impotent, crushed by the dark mass of worries. The nightmare only stops when daylight filters through the shutters, the bells ring from some public building, the apartment building shakes itself like a drowsy animal. Light is an ally. It's a euphoric moment when you realise you've come through after a night on the edge of the abyss. Getting up brings a calmness won out

17 *Compagnie Républicaine de Sécurité* – the French riot police.

of terror. I only have to stand up to be ready to face the world. I was dead and now I'm alive again.

I fill these barren hours by making use of them: I polish sentences in my head, I keep long novels on hand to read, no tome however massive can hold out against long, sleepless nights, I watch horror films, my favourite genre since adolescence. They have a soothing power: the ravenous zombies delight me, the criminal psychopaths calm me down, the impact of the ice-axe on the victim's skull seems as delicate as the clink of a spoon opening a soft-boiled egg. I tremble to be released from my fear, knowing for certain that at the end I will finally be able to close my eyes. Anything rather than the hell of futile clear-sightedness, of sterile hyperactivity. Or I view cartoon films in the hope that this mild regression will help me recover a child's capacity for sleep.

Sometimes a miracle happens, an idea surfaces in the nocturnal calm, a plot forms thanks to the cerebral turbulence. But that blessing is rare, the dust and ashes produced by a mind near the end of its tether and the creative sparks of the insomniac are as meaningless as the pseudo-genius imparted by drugs. However, I will never give up: like the Ancient Greeks and Romans I know that sleep is not a minor art but testimony to one's quality of life. The rarest thing that can happen to me is to realise that I've had a good night's sleep after all and don't need any more. I get so excited about this that I don't close an eye for nights on end.

When I was an adolescent for a long time I had a bizarre dream: I was running away from home in short trousers and jumped into the lift shaft but invariably a witch with claw-like fingernails would catch me by the braces and make me come back up, like a yoyo. As she hoisted me up, I shrank and returned home almost an infant again. I am the child pulled back by his braces whenever he tries to take off and free himself from his heritage. The witch's finger is the tie of blood, the laws of heredity, the weight of memory, of genetics – no matter what explanation is given, the finger holds me back and makes whatever people want of me, always a son and a son of. To emancipate yourself is to tear yourself away from your origins while still taking them on.

'Never forget you're Jewish,' Alain Finkielkraut's mother would tell him.

'Never forget where you come from,' my parents would tell me again and again, like an echo.

That meant: stay modest and above all don't deny us. I would retort, 'We belong to the world we've made, not to the one we come from.'

'Stop trying to be clever!'

By an unexpected dialectical process my father unwittingly Judaïsed me, adding his own son to the list of his hereditary enemies. If I were to trace the ancestry of this misunderstanding I would see its origin in our surname that is both Jewish and Protestant. My father used to claim that the Jewish Bruckners wrote their name with a diaeresis over the 'u' while we didn't: so two little dots separated the sheep from the goats, a barrier which, I'm sure you'll agree, is pretty thin. Later on I learnt that a René Bruckner had been shot as a Jew by the Germans in August 1944 at Lyon-Bron Airport. He had been living in Lyons, was born in 1921, the same year as my father, and had the same name as him – a disturbing homonym. My spontaneous reaction was to immediately identify with the people he detested. A psychoanalyst would say I was seeking to atone for my father's hatred and there's no doubt about that: it's not mere chance that for thirty years I've been working on the guilt of the West and the twists-and-turns of repentance.

My first publications immediately installed me along with Bernard-Henri Lévy and André Glucksman in the ranks of the new philosophers, thus placing me on the list of Jewish intellectuals. That is the title under which I'm still reviewed today on Google by the supporters of the extreme right and Islamic fanatics. When I try to refute this, people shake their heads sceptically: 'No problem, we respect your choice.' With a laugh a friend said, 'You ought to come out, goy.'

For many people I have become a reverse Marrano, a renegade hated as a Zionist, an unconditional lackey of Israel and the United States, constantly forced to explain my background. This *de facto* situation is the result of chance as much as of an unconscious choice: finally to become an object of execration for my father, the bodily incarnation of what he hated most. I've had to undo the threads of this ideological brain-washing bit by bit. It began with Vladimir Jankélévitch, my professor at the Sorbonne, of Russian origin. My father's comment on him was entirely predictable: 'What a pity all these brilliant men are Jews!'

In 1971 I did a master's dissertation under him about '*The Myth of Degeneracy in National Socialism*', even then determined to purge myself of years of family propaganda by going directly to the documents. Happening to refer to Daniel Guérin, a militant homosexual, I was told by my outraged mother that after the Liberation, in September 1944, he had denounced my maternal grandmother to the committee of the 5th arrondissement in Paris. This woman, of natural distinction and great strength of mind, had dared to leave her husband during the 1930s and bring up her nine children on her own; she had left when the tenth arrived – fortunately a miscarriage. Close to Princess Marthe Bibesco, a writer of Romanian origin, she ran a bookshop as well as a boarding house in the Rue de l'Esplanade, where several officers of the *Wehrmacht* had stayed. She was saved by the testimony of a Polish journalist, whom she had hidden during the Occupation. A nice example of balance. I can still hear Jankélévitch, after my dissertation had been accepted with some comments on details, pointing out to me in his surprisingly young-sounding, staccato voice, like that of Jean-Pierre Léaud in Truffaut's films, how abstract my thesis was: 'It's OK, Bruckner, but it sounds as if you're discussing the quarrel about universals. There's not much passion in your study. You've got to get involved, my lad, after all, it's still a burning issue.'

He certainly had style, that intellectual *condottiere* with his magnificently tousled hair, his long grey forelock framing the outline of his face, turning him into a Romantic hero who had strayed into our century. He hadn't succumbed to the proletarian sloppiness of dress that was the uniform of the time, especially at Vincennes University: unkempt hair, pullover with holes, shirt hanging out, a glimpse of tummy, the eternal baggy jeans, unpolished shoes. The shapeless generation. There was a magnetism about him that carried me away and when he played the piano for us in his apartment on the Quai aux Fleurs, a piece by Liszt or Ravel, I had the feeling I was in a novel by Turgenev or Chekhov. Elegance: the maximum intensity with the minimum effect. He would scrutinise me closely, seeking to penetrate my shell. I would shiver, so much did I admire him. If he were to learn the truth about my family, I would fall into disgrace, I would lose his esteem for good! Then, as so often, I concealed my uneasiness beneath a façade of casualness.

Nowadays, for example, reading on an Islamo-fascist site that I'm 'a sly Jew who's sold out to his Yankee masters, a lackey of the Zionist organisation' gives me a kind of dismal pleasure. It's a spit in the face that I take as a compliment. It's an awkward situation this partly double identity. I know some Gentiles who, feeling the need to show solidarity with a minority, celebrate Yom Kippur, Hanukkah, Pesach. Too kosher for some, not enough for others, I feel I'm permanently trying to keep my balance, oscillating between a sense of imposture and the delights of ambiguity. I'm pleased to have corrupted our surname from the inside, to have bound it, despite myself, to the family of Moses. I'm happy to be a usurper. I've always dreamt of the fate of Mr. Klein, played by Alain Delon in Losey's film of the same name, who is caught in a round-up of Jews during the war and goes along with it, even though he's not a Jew. Or else I have a puerile fantasy of being a saviour: passing a synagogue, I protect the children from a crazed killer who wants to annihilate them. How often have I said to my father, just to annoy him, 'You know everyone thinks I'm Jewish?'

'That's a terrible lie,' he fumed.

'There are Bruckners without the diaeresis on the wall of the deportees of the Shoah Memorial in Paris, in the sixth arrondissement.'

'They just happen to sound the same.'

'You know your granddaughter Anna's Jewish as well?'

His face sagged. He was boxed in. In 1983 or 1984 he'd sent a letter to the satirical magazine *Crapouillot* that had mistakenly included me in the category of Jewish French writers. For years he was to inundate editorial offices with letters correcting the error every time I was listed under the wrong rubric. And when I introduced him to my latest partner Rihanna, a mixed-race woman of Belgian/Rwandan background with a Tutsi mother and a Jewish-Hungarian father, grand-niece of the last king of Rwanda, Kigeli V who was exiled in Washington, he hissed,

‘If it amuses you, that’s your problem.’

His own blood was betraying him. He’d dreamt of a Valkyrie, what he got was a mulatto. To comfort himself he went through the highways and by-ways of genealogy with her, explaining that she wasn’t African but Nilotic (from the Nile region, like the Egyptians) and he was reassured by the fact that her skin was relatively light, depending on the time of day, pale in the morning, dark in the evening. She listened to him politely, though with an ironic expression, and reminded him that her mother, who came from Kivu in the east of the Congo, was a great African lady who could hardly speak French. He told my Italian-Slovene daughter-in-law, my son’s partner, that she should forget her ‘dialect’ and speak solely Italian or German, the only worthwhile languages of eastern Europe; moreover Slovenia, a southern province of the Austrian Empire, ought to be restored to the mother country and the whole of eastern Europe should be put under the control of either Germany or Russia. Fortunately his heart was stronger than his prejudices, he was a loving and generous grandfather. As soon as it was a matter of personal relations, he would cut the emotional domain off from his own opinions and could show true openness.

Am I any better than my parents? I’ve avoided their mistakes but I’ve made different ones. I’ve taken so much care not to repeat their errors that I didn’t see those lying in wait for me. I have dedicated my life entirely to books, perhaps to the detriment of human beings. Like many men of my generation, at twenty I was a rather spasmodic father for my son, only to turn into a doting father with my daughter at forty-seven. As an altar boy of a cult that is in the process of disappearing – that of the book at a time when ignorance is becoming militant – I sometimes see myself as the hero of *Bidochon*, the comic strip by Binet: in a vulgar, narrow-minded and chauvinistic family, Kador, a learned dog, secretly reads philosophy books, with a predilection for Kant's *Critique of Pure Reason*, while he's eating his dog food. When his master catches him reading this 'trash', he gives him a good hiding and forces him to watch television with 'Maman' Raymonde. The dog sighs at the vulgarity of his masters and dreams of going back to the beauty of philosophical speculation. On the train, the bus or the plane, where everyone's tapping away at their tablet or smartphone, I feel like that scolded doggie, terribly old-fashioned with my books and jotters.

It's endurance that makes the artist, the will to persevere despite doubts and repudiation. I practise a profession that's close to voluntary confinement. To write is to shut oneself away. One's study is a prison that opens the gates to freedom. As a child I loved the retreats in monasteries, the long hours of meditation and prayer, the effect of which was to intensify the silence. Now I have the Trappist monastery inside myself, I have my cell at home where I cloister myself for the whole day, only going out to see my my fellow men and women in the evening. If I have unravelled a difficulty, finished a page, I think myself the most fortunate of men. I get up in the morning to Bach cantatas, the sole convincing proof of the existence of God, as someone quite rightly said. Ensconced in my sanctum, working to music, at ease in the proximity of the thousands of volumes surrounding me, I feel incredibly privileged. Just as an author shuts himself away to write, he dreams of seeing his books out on shelves, on the sand of a beach or the seat of a train. There is no greater tribute for him than to have provided a pretext for two lovers to meet, burning with desire. A book is made to be read, forgotten or passed on according to the laws of chance. We create confined, we only exist dispersed.

Chapter 7

The Virulence of the Widower

A life had flown by, a rather happy one for me. I hadn't seen my father for years and I didn't miss him. I had consigned him to ancient history. We occasionally had brief telephone conversations, my mother tried to bring us together but I had nothing to say to him. My successes annoyed and pleased him in equal part: they contradicted all his prejudices. I remember his thinly veiled disappointment when I told him over the telephone that I'd been given a literary prize for my novel *Les Voleurs de beauté* (*The Thieves of Beauty*). He asked me if the vote hadn't been rigged; was the award truly merited? Whatever the case, he wasn't interested in the book. The old grouch could still deliver his venom. When, after a long illness, my mother died in 1999, I found myself, unshielded, facing an old man who had become a stranger. I was so sure he was going to disappear that I was at a loss what to do when I was landed with him, still pretty sprightly at over eighty. I had the impression I'd been carried back to my native soil, to the mediocrity of family life. It was like returning to a province that's been abandoned but is still malignant. I became a shackled son once more. After all those fathers in spirit who had stretched me, my biological father, small now, was reasserting his rights. He assured me that he would never get over the death of my mother. I was sceptical, perhaps wrongly so. I underestimated the profound attachment uniting them despite everything. They'd been like two wasps in a jar trying to sting each other to death but at least they'd agreed to share the same jar.

Meanwhile he'd suffered several financial setbacks: after twenty years going up the social scale, he'd fallen into a spiral of debt like his father who, the heir to a prosperous manufacturer, had ended up destitute, in the poorhouse of the 20th arrondissement. Risky investments, excessive purchases, younger and therefore expensive mistresses – in brief a minor delusion of grandeur – had left him, at retirement age, in financial difficulties. Through his relative affluence he had lost all sense of moderation. Having worked his way laboriously up to the middle class he was tumbling down at top speed into the lower classes. He brooded over failed ambitions, career fantasies. For years he'd been living from hand to mouth, on loans at extortionate rates from criminal organisations. Hardly had he opened a bank account than he was wondering about the amount of the authorised overdraft. He just about kept going by sponging off dupes or occasional benefactors whom he hoped would pull him out of the mire of debt. Some of them had had the good grace to die before repayment was due. He'd scrounged off the members of the family, one after the other, while insulting them behind their backs. By imperceptible degrees the lender would be transformed into a bastard, illustrating the famous law of ingratitude: 'I have no enemies, I've not given anyone a helping hand.' (Jules Renard)

Having drained my uncles and aunts dry, he turned to me; basing his argument on my success, he hoped that in repayment for the expenses he'd incurred for my education, I would make him an allowance until he died. We haggled over my largesse like a pair of hucksters but I hadn't the heart to leave him in the red. So that was another grievance to add to my list, and not the least either. Every two or three months he would demand his pittance and I would cough up grudgingly. He lived on handouts, all the while inveighing against beggars, immigrants, people on benefits. Shameless, he even went so far as to demand a bit of cash from his grandson. The whole of my family, on both my mother's and my father's side, showed a cupidity worthy of a novel by Balzac: their hatred of the Jews was all the greater because they projected our very French passion for money onto them. The night when my maternal grandmother died, her two elder daughters came to blows, over her still warm body, in order to carry off a table or a piece of furniture. My father left in the early hours with a pair of chairs, arguing that his late mother-in-law had promised him them. The smaller the nest egg, the more ravenous the mourners.

In 1969 he'd bought a ruined mill in Saint-Saturnin-lès-Apt in the Luberon, well before the region became the preferred holiday region of the Parisian intelligentsia. After his *Sturm und Drang*, his Nazi Storm and Stress, he dreamt, inspired by the *Félibrige*,[18] of putting down roots in the Midi and saw himself, as his fiftieth decade began, as a Provençal gentleman-farmer. He played the local, having registered in the Vaucluse Department. The mill, that was to be his great work, his social stamp of approval, became his shroud and he sold it for a song thirty-five years later, leaving behind an unsightly building, infested with mice, beside a minor road.

---

18 Frédéric Mistral wrote in the Occitan language of southern France and, with other writers, founded the *Félibrige* to promote the language and culture of the region.

He had hired the services of an alcoholic gardener, a decent guy whom he insulted and threatened to hit. This hired hand was the husband of a woman who ran a little hotel-cum-brothel for long-distance lorry drivers between Gordes and the hamlet of Les Bassacs. With her crew-cut hair and docker's physique the madam, who had been on the game herself in Marseilles, looked like a Sumo wrestler with a Marseillais accent. She granted my father permission to treat him roughly, even to knock him about if necessary. She would help out in the unauthorised brothel herself when there was a rush and finish off the clients who were in the greatest hurry. My father regularly went to eat in the truck stop and would have sex with the two or three girls who worked there on a rota system. When he was annoyed, he would take it out on the poor guy, who would be so distressed he would cry. My mother warned him he was in danger of getting clouted with a fork or spade in reprisal. Eventually the gardener died from advanced cirrhosis of the liver. The brothel was closed down and the police even came to question my father. As an habitué he had been a character witness for the owner, who was stuck in Baumettes Prison in Marseilles. My mother, who told me all this many years later, suffered a double indignity: to learn that her husband used the local brothel and that he was, moreover, suspected by the authorities of taking a cut of the profits of the business. No proceedings were taken against him, but in a restaurant in Geneva he almost managed to get his face smashed in by two gallows-birds: they were flanking one of the former girls from the Provençal whorehouse whom he had gone over to greet like an old fellow-student.

At that time he had done a left turn, let his hair grow longer, voted for Mitterrand or even the communists. After all, the rest of the family was working-class, card-carrying members of the Party and the trade union. He was always grateful to the socialist president for having flowers put on the grave of Marshal Pétain on the Île d'Yeu every year. Did even my mother not shed a tear at the fall of the Wall, arguing that it left no more obstacles to the spread of capitalism? This ideological volatility with pendulum swings from one extreme to the other is characteristic of our confused age. There was the occasional outburst of anti-Semitism, like a fit of political hiccoughs. People would say, 'Hey, it's coming back,' then it was gone again.

My father cultivated his neo-rural persona, invented Occitan origins; seeking a new identity, he joined groups protecting the natural environment, was sympathetic to the Friends of the Earth which, he said, 'doesn't lie,' and the French Farmers' Confederation for its struggles against agribusiness and American fast food. He drifted from one substitute faith of the times to another: liberalism, ecology, regionalism, the sexual revolution. Henry Miller had made a sensational entry into the house along with Teilhard de Chardin and his omega point. Louis Pauwels' review *Planète*[19] replaced *Rivarol,* the fanatical and demonic Theosophist Gurdjieff supplanted Brasillach. My father even went to visit Lanza del Vasto, the militant, non-violent pacifist and disciple of Ghandi who had founded the Community of the Ark near Lodève in Languedoc; he was impressed by it and couldn't stop talking about the inner beauty and magnetism of the friend of Romain Rolland. He also took the opportunity to buy the works of Luc Dietrich and René Daumal.[20] It seemed a

19 A bi-monthly devoted to fantastic realism with the slogan: 'Nothing that's strange is alien to us.'

20 Dietrich (1913–1944) and Daumal (1908–1944) were two writers whose works explored spirituality.

complete metamorphosis, taking him from the raging dictator to a mystical poet. Impossible to imagine a greater gulf. His work as an engineer often took him to the Mahgreb where he went into raptures about the Algerian success and the mistakes France made during the colonial period, blaming de Gaulle for not having granted independence immediately in 1958. He'd undergone a complete change! He became the advocate of Franco-German reconciliation, supporting Joseph Rovan and Alfred Grosser.[21] He even held a grudge against the English and Americans for not having bombed Auschwitz, accused the GIs of having committed abundant rape in Normandy and condemned the Vietnam War; in brief he joined the left-wing anti-Americanism after having espoused that of the extreme right wing. Thus he embraced the whole of the political spectrum, which allowed him to prolong his old vituperation whilst appearing to have reinvented himself.

As old age approached, he developed diabetes that he attributed to me even though he was drinking and eating too much. Retirement was a tragedy for him; he felt he'd been thrown on the scrapheap and every day he wrote dozens of letters in his spidery scrawl seeking employment again, putting forward his skills, his knowledge of German. His aggressive onslaughts were pointless exercises, there was no one there to torment any more, my mother was nothing but an empty shell out of which he'd torn the life. There are two aspects to financial difficulties: for young people there is hope. They compel them to work hard, restrict their wishes, try to

21 Joseph Rovan (1908–1944) although born in Germany, was a French philosopher; he was Jewish but converted to Catholicism and, despite having been incarcerated in Dachau, was influential in encouraging reconciliation with Germany. Alfred Grosser (b. 1925) is a French-German writer who made a great contribution to French-German cooperation after 1945.

outdo others in intelligence and imagination. The later one, that confronts people in their sixties following relative success and when spending money has become a habit, is more cruel. It's a slow decline after their great hopes, a drop in status. My father used to spend money in order to forget he was poor. Now my parents had to move house every five years and every apartment was half the size of the previous one. After having started at Porte d'Auteuil in the sixteenth arrondissement, they finished in a one-room flat on Rue Cabanais, opposite Sainte-Anne Hospital, where my mother, as my father said in his charming way, would only have to cross the road to get her deranged mind treated. He had one final passionate relationship: he fell in love with a young woman in Eygalières, a small village in the Bouches-du Rhône, Provence. He was seriously smitten, ready to give up everything for her. My mother, sensing danger, rang the lady in question and, with threats, revealed that her aged lover was stony broke and could not provide for a future together with her. For months on end my father would sob in bed at the loss of his beloved, who wasn't even beautiful, from what he said – he liked ugly women for their hidden charms. I've always been moved by the thought of that old man shedding tears in the arms of his lawful wedded wife at the loss of his mistress.

Then there was the saga of his food supplies. His diary for 1941–1944 is full of restaurant menus copied out, of searches for butter, sugar, cheese. A dinner of snails washed down with Pouilly-Fumé at a Youth Work Camp in 1941 led to a page full of lyrical notes. Getting something to eat was his major concern. In my parents' conversation the Second World War was reduced to their obsession with food. No meat – offal, thin soup and swedes, Jerusalem artichokes, broth made with chestnuts, chicory, ersatz coffee. They had no room for the sufferings of others, they'd had their own ration of deprivation. At home the cupboards were full of preserves, of rice and pasta. At every international crisis – the Bay of Pigs, Suez, the Algiers *putsch* – my father would arrive home with the boot stuffed full of imperishable items of food. Every two or three years he got ready to survive a siege. We spent long winter evenings preparing jars of peaches, pears, jam, at which he was very good. They rotted away on the shelves, solidified into deposits of sugar. I've kept a jar of redcurrants, an unbreakable block of anthracite that I contemplate like the remnant of a civilisation that has disappeared. When he died, the removal men found more than 300 jars in his cellar.

So you had to eat, eat all the time: soup, vegetables and, above all, meat, that was a categorical imperative, good meat oozing with blood that strengthened your bones. At four o'clock I was given a slice of bread covered with a thick layer of butter sprinkled with cocoa. And that's not counting the daily glass of milk, called Mendès-France milk after the name of the prime minister who in 1954 arranged for the drink to be distributed in schools, to the fury of home distillers and Pierre Poujade, who suspected he 'didn't have one single drop of Gallic blood in his veins.' In this Poujade was unknowingly parodying Charles Maurras[22] who insisted that a Jew, not being rooted in the soil of France, would never be capable of understanding Racine's verse.

When we lived in Lyons my father would take trips to Switzerland, the land of milk and honey, and would return weighed down with Gruyere, *Appenzeller*, chocolates, after

22 1868–1952. French writer and one of the founders of the nationalist *Action Française*; some of his ideas were close to the Nazi 'blood and soil' philosophy.

having devoured a cheese fondue on the way. Should he go to El Aaiún in the Western Sahara to work for the Moroccan Phosphate Commission he would return with five kilos of French beans. To Germany? Sausages and *sauerkraut*, Rhine wine, *Schwarzbrot, Pumpernickel* (dark rye bread). Our larder in the cellar was full to overflowing. We regularly had to throw out the surplus that had gone bad from the heat or been nibbled at by the cockroaches. Even when he was young my father would get up during the night to make himself an omelette, some sauté potatoes. Watching him eat took away my appetite: he would gobble his food down with shiny lips, fill his belly, going bright red. When my mother and I commented on this, he would retort, 'Shut your gob, I'm starving.'

He was fat, swollen like a balloon. Most people in our family would finish their meals with crimson cheeks, purplish complexion, heated by the drinks and the food. I felt ashamed of this, associating it with peasant origins, and as soon as I felt my face start to burn, take on a purple tinge, I would leave the table and go to refresh myself, go to my mother's bathroom and put on some powder to make my skin whiter. I wanted to be pale, ashen.

Until his final year my father would come right across Paris to arrive at my flat with a shopping basket full of bottles of olive oil, fruit, old cheeses, hunks of bread. I was touched by this and waited until he had left to throw three quarters of it away. Haunted by the idea of shortages, he would collect all the little sachets of sugar lying about on café tables; they ended up in his pockets, infested with ants and fleas. He had made dealing with leftovers into a fine art. When he was in hospital I had to take him fruit and jars of jam, even bottles of wine that he stashed away behind his bedside table and that the nursing auxiliaries tolerated. I wouldn't have been surprised if he'd asked for victuals to be put in his coffin, just in case Jesus and Saint Peter should be short in the world beyond.

To grow up is to invent your own life: to get old is to deduce it from several earlier principles. If your choices have been wrong ones, your old age will be in their image. My father survived my mother by thirteen years, living until he was ninety-two, gradually declining without his mind ever going, still fit as a fiddle, aggressive, ranting and raving. He came to resemble Jean-Marie Le Pen more and more, as if his appearance were dictated by his opinions. He would ramble on, dragging up family quarrels from forty years ago. There was always an unworthy uncle, a shabby sister-in-law, nephews who were failures. They were all kept in a sort of inexhaustible box of moans from which he would take out new grievances every day. Old habits from a life of work die hard: he would be up at six in the morning and exhausted from eight, waiting for lunch slumped in front of the television on at full blast. This wishy-washy visual diet would keep him going until the evening. I suggested he should undertake some social task, make himself useful to the community. He shrugged his shoulders and grumbled, 'Get stuck with a load of other doddery old men helping scroungers, no thanks.'

As I said, at the hospital where my mother was dying he met a former mistress who herself was visiting her husband who was nearing the end. Single again, the two got together and stayed together for twelve years. She was a former lawyer who 'shared his ideas'. I was pleased with this companionship that brightened his old age, he wrote to her almost every day, long hand-written missives in French or German that I sometimes posted for him. He was sincerely in love with her. He would spend half the week with her in her huge apartment in the 16th arrondissement where he had his own room. They went to Australia together and adored it: at least a country, he told me when he came back, where there were 'neither negroes nor Arabs,' just hard-working Chinese. As for the Jews, 'they keep their heads down and their traps shut.'

Above all I dreaded having him on my hands, having to take him in: we would have killed each other within 24 hours. I used to invite him to lunch in my apartment. These visits caused me mental anguish: he wouldn't leave but stayed there, silent, in his disaster zone, looking miserable, his face twisted in a bitter scowl as if our agitation were an insult to his sorrow. Like many old people he was prey to fits of automatic mastication that I found exasperating; I would ask him to control himself, I felt like cementing his jaws to immobilise them. He hated my split-level apartment because it hadn't got a lift, nor a room for him: everything offended him, the pictures on the wall he'd liked to slash, the furniture, the stairs that were too steep, a little Dutch clock with the movement taken out that he had to restrain himself not to crush in his hands. But he remained there as if rooted to the spot and I hadn't the heart to throw him out, especially when he'd been articulate, well-informed, surprising us with his knowledge of wines and food.

Around 2007 there was a technical misunderstanding that could have had serious consequences. I'd gone for a lecture tour to India, a country about which my father, who'd never been there, had a decided opinion: 'They'll never get anywhere with their sacred cows and their castes.'

I sent him an SMS on his landline – he couldn't read messages on his mobile. The text is supposed to be read by a synthetic voice. I'd written, 'Journey fine. Everything's OK. Kisses.' But the voice cut off the last syllable so that instead of

'*Je t'embrasse*' he heard it as '*Je t'aime*' – 'I love you.' He was deeply moved by it, his partner told me. I was embarrassed but couldn't take it back. The fatal word, much too weighty, had been said. He was decent enough to forget this erroneous declaration. We celebrated his eighty-eighth birthday at the Closerie des Lilas, with my daughter. He'd got himself up elegantly, it was a good moment. He arrived ahead of time, ate and drank with a good appetite – starter, main course, dessert, liqueur – and left on the bus. I found myself thinking, with a touch of admiration, 'He's indestructible.'

I forced myself to ring him every day to hear how he was doing. My instability in matters of the heart worried him. I explained to him that, like some other people, I sway between the need for security and the need for freedom: when I'm alone, I dream of conjugal togetherness, as one of a couple I have the feeling I'm being asphyxiated, I keep coming up against the bars of a cell. Eventually I've become accustomed to this oscillation and I've given up trying to get rid of it, seeing in the non-resolution the charm of a possible solution. To the end I will remain in search of an ideal state halfway between celibacy and living together with someone. My arguments didn't convince him at all. 'You'll grow old alone,' he muttered. Sometimes a miracle did happen. We came together in our appreciation of several authors he absolutely revered: Maupassant, Zola, Daphne du Maurier. He could discuss them intelligently. He also adored Irène Nemirovsky, for reasons that were less clear to me, because, according to his interpretation, she 'was ashamed of being a Jew and showed no hatred of the French.' Above all it was through him that I discovered that extraordinary novella by Villiers de l'Isle Adam, *La Torture par l'espérance* (*Torture by Hope*), the story of a Dominican attached to the Inquisition in Toledo who pretends to liberate a rabbi, allowing him to flee out into the country so as to be able to catch him in the nick of time and have him burnt at the stake while promising him he'll be in paradise that very evening. Even today I still can't understand what attracted him to the story: the unctuous sadism of the Dominican or the bewilderment of the rabbi, duped in order to intensify his punishment.

Most of the time he only had one mode of expression: indignation. The filthiness of Paris, dog dirt on the pavement, beggars, Roma, young people, road hogs all outraged him more than a massacre in the Middle East or a disaster in Africa. Everything hurts this man of great age: he's superfluous, dependant on everyone, and is on the lookout for signs of impatience to be rid of him in the expressions of his nearest and dearest. The least technological innovation or linguistic fad sends him back into bygone years. He holds it against the whole of humanity that it's going to survive him, society is pushing him towards the exit. A simple flight of steps in the *métro* is an expedition for him, demanding a huge effort. The new longevity promised by medicine is also a curse. People are getting old at the same time as their parents and sometimes more quickly than them. They're still there, hoary, creaking, while you're already a grandfather. The modern world is creating dynasties of old folks in more or less advanced states of decrepitude, families of bedridden ancients assisted by other old people who are their children, equally wrinkled, bowed – every stage of Methuselah. Our parents and grandparents are mankind's emissaries from the upper spheres of age. They tell us one simple fact: life is still possible. Whether it's desirable is quite a different matter.

There is no doubt that nastiness is a good preservative. At Charbonnières, on the outskirts of Lyons, we had two neighbours, a mother and daughter. The mother, who had cancer that developed slowly and took ages to finish her off, persecuted her child with unbridled ferocity. There were furious outbursts until late into the night and, above all, thrashings with a stick, a whip. The poor young woman, vainly hoping for a man who would rescue her from this hell, fell ill. The old woman would wake her up in the middle of the night, forcing her to wash the floor, iron clothes. At dinner we could hear her through the party wall screaming, 'I should have had an abortion, should have drowned you like a kitten when you were born, you useless bitch.'

My mother would close the window, trembling. The daughter, haggard and gaunt, not allowed to talk to us without authorisation, wasted away and died. The brute of a mother continued to castigate her, even on her deathbed. She survived her by several years and we could hear her screaming during the night, in the empty house, giving vent to her loathing of the daughter whom she had only brought into the world the better to kill her.

Throughout my childhood, hearing the cries of that witch I was haunted by one obsessive fear: of dying young. My mother had predicted it so often. Every time I had a temperature or an infection, I would tell myself, 'This time you've had it.' When I was twenty-one and in hospital with an internal haemorrhage as a result of gastric perforation, my father came into the ward and announced, 'You're paying for your dissolute life. Keep on like that and you won't live to be more than thirty.'

I chucked him out, but his comment had struck home. There were lots of adjectives my way of life deserved, only not 'dissolute', alas. For the next ten years I would wake up in the morning afraid I wouldn't last out till the evening. Today I'm not interested in my death, inevitable and unpleasant as it will be. The only deaths that count are those of people dear to you, who have always gone too soon. A little petition to Providence: see that I disappear before those I love, don't make me have to bear the guilt of the survivor.

Right up to his end my father pretended to be worried about me. I couldn't stand his solicitude, it was his insidious way of wishing me harm while pretending to be concerned. He was like those sanctimonious hypocrites who prowl round other people's misfortune, licking their lips, to feast on it. He would have liked me to fall ill so he'd feel less alone. As soon as I entered his room, he'd scrutinise me with a sour expression on his face, 'I must say you look a bit under the weather.'

'No, not at all. I'm fine.'

'Well you look awful, if you don't mind my saying so.'

'Have you looked at yourself?'

He didn't like my books, he thought them too long, too laboured, too complicated, too one-track. Whenever I committed myself to a cause or headed off to some distant destination – Africa, Asia or Latin America – he would try to discourage me. 'Don't go wasting your time on those morons! What on earth are you up to with those flea-ridden down-and-outs.'

I didn't have a permanent position. Every time there was a change of government he'd ask me:

'They haven't offered offered you a post?'

'They have, as president, but I refused.'

He would go on at me, 'Be polite to so-and-so, you might need him some day.'

To annoy him I would call him after a hike in the mountains or when I'd been out jogging. I would puff and pant vigorously so he could sense the energy driving me and his own stasis.

'Oh, Papa, I really feel fit.'

'Yes, but be careful you don't get a coronary.'

His imminent death gave me a fierce desire to live.

'You can keep your lousy happiness,' my mother said to me one day when I was in too cheerful a mood for her taste. Whenever I told her, 'Everything's fine,' she would interpret it as meaning, 'I've no need of you.'

One afternoon my father and I met at Denfert-Rochereau, there were some papers I had to pass on to him. We sat down in a café. As usual the conversation quickly dried up; we had little to say to each other while my mother and I could chat fluently for hours, about all kinds of things. If a moment comes when everything has been said between two people, a sort of ice paralyses the bubbling spring of language. It was in October, the weather still fine and mild. I watched the women pass by, so smart, so varied, finding some comfort in their wake. Whether all the misery-guts like it or not, the mixing of races in our towns has considerably enriched the range of what is on offer to the eye. For me the sight of all these elegant women from all kinds of racial backgrounds was a counterweight to the infirm old man. His face was frozen in a rancorous expression. After an amply proportioned young black woman had passed close to our table, my father wheezed, 'Aren't people ugly. Just look at that huge backside. How can they traipse round like that?'

I leant over to him, irritated by his remark that was aimed directly at me. 'You know, Papa, there are men who adore big arses. It's all a question of taste.'

'Well you're welcome to them.'

'These people are beautiful, Papa, it's your eyes that are ugly.'

I sent a silent prayer to heaven: see that I never become like him. May my children finish me off if I'm ever going to end up like that. The worst thing about old age is not the physical decrease, it's the disgust with mankind. How many start off as subversives only to finish as grouches? Rebels at twenty, bellyachers at sixty. My father brought me up to execrate other people, I have chosen to celebrate them.The beauty of the world and its creatures will never cease to amaze me.

Chapter 8

You Ought to do a Stefan Zweig

I've never known what a successful life looks like; on the other hand I can very well tell what a detestable life is like. In the evening of his life, when he should have been lowering his guard, taking stock, my father found new fury. For him December became a new spring. Abhorrence was what gave him the energy to remain alive, to keep going. At that point his racialist passion returned with increased virulence due to his financial difficulties. The embers of his Judaeophobia were still smouldering, all it needed was a gust of wind to set them on fire again. This return to the Nazism of his youth, after a long gap, was perhaps a way of defeating time. If he had admitted he was wrong, like those despairing communists after the fall of the Wall in 1989, he would have fallen into a state of despondency, his life would have turned into a long cul-de-sac. He preferred to see himself as the guardian of a truth unheard in a world won over to delusion.

At every minor health problem he would say to the doctors, 'I've the right to live to a hundred, you know. It's up to you to keep me fit.'

He'd become a burden, causing me anger and a guilty conscience. I decided to play the dutiful son despite everything. If I'd abandoned him I wouldn't have been able to look myself in the mirror. My sense of guilt revived an intermittent affection. There comes a moment when relations with a person are so mixed up one can no longer distinguish love from duty. I detested my father, there was no doubt about that, but not every day. My solicitude disturbed him, he sensed a hint of the Grim Reaper behind it. But if I didn't call him, he felt he'd been abandoned. I would go to see him, in his flat in Rue Cabanais. I would hammer at the door – he was deaf. He couldn't hear anything except the ring of the telephone and he would lift the receiver even when it was ringing on the television. The television is the real family of old and sick people, it's an untiring companion that always has something to say and to show. His one-room flat was abominable: the walls were peeling, the ceiling was mottled with huge stains. The table, broken in the middle as if by a blow from an axe, was covered with papers, left-over food, various medicines. He'd made little mounds of these things, like prehistorical tumuli with cockroaches wandering round among them. As a good geographer he'd drawn tracks in the dust, made junctions.

'Oh, these cockroaches, you know, are a sign of cleanliness. They're extremely meticulous insects, they'd never go into the house of someone who's dirty.'

The kitchen was priceless: cluttered with pans, greyish hunks of bread, spilt coffee, dried-out teabags. Various kinds of stewed fruit were slowly rotting in their juice, meat stews going green in the middle of winter – he forbade me to throw them away. As soon as I came in, I would hold my nose demonstratively and read the riot act: 'Aren't you ashamed to live in this pigsty?'

It was his favourite thing to say whenever he came into my room when I was a child. He looked frightened. 'But you're mistaken, Pascal, it's very clean.'

That brought a lump to my throat. I offered to pay for a home help, which he accepted in his final year. I suggested I come with my son to give the place a good spring clean, we'd wash the rooms down thoroughly, bring in professional decorators to do up the place, especially the bathroom that was half an undertaker's, half a municipal lavatory: 'Give me 48 hours and I'll have it as good as new.'

He flatly refused. It wasn't his responsibility to have the ceiling repainted, it was the city council's. Like Job, he'd fallen in love with his own dunghill. He didn't see it any more. Never throw anything away, never lose anything, not even a *métro* ticket, that was his rule from then on. Any piece of wood or metal, however small, that he found in the street, he would put on one side. You never knew. Like his own father at the end of his life, he rummaged through bins, took out bits of toys, pieces of Meccano. The curse of rubbish fell on him in his turn. Stuck at home by himself, he kept fifty-year old files including the copies of letters he'd written 'just in case'. Above all, he was afraid of thefts, of the hordes of burglars who'd put him at the top of their list. He saw himself as a wealthy man surrounded by a gang of robbers.

I really let him have it: 'You've nothing to steal but junk. Just look round you, for God's sake! You're living in a pile of shit, d'you hear. What language do you want me to tell you that in?'

The cleaning woman, a Moroccan, had to pass a veritable exam plus a morality test, as if she were being engaged to serve His Highness. The Great Panjandrum was looking for staff. References were demanded! But he grew fond of her, gave her coffee, liqueurs, wanted to crack open the champagne on any pretext, talked to her about Morocco and his love of the country. She quickly became indispensable to him. She gave me horrendous reports on the hygiene of the lavatory; for certain tasks she wore gloves and a mask. The bathroom and toilet, black with filth, were unfit for use, permeated with a suffocating smell. On his bed, that was never made, were soft toys – bears, rabbits, foxes – and this menagerie sat facing the devotional photo, stuck to the wall, of Marshal Pétain. The soft toys, if you could believe him, belonged to a game between his last partner and himself. I didn't want to know any more about that. She had come to see him once and rang me up, nauseated. His tiny flat had become a tip. He reminded me of those fossilised beings stuck in a pavement corner, like saints in their niches. He'd made himself a cave in his fortress of rubbish. He would sit there like some deposed king on his throne of debris. After his death we found the skeleton of a chicken in his freezer, nothing but bones, at least two years old. The skeleton, with shards of ice as ballast, proffered its rigging to the worst of the weather as it continued on its journey through time. It could have remained frozen in the icefield for years.

Diabetes was eating away at his legs, disrupting the circulation of the blood, the toes of his left foot were gangrenous, they cut off one then two and three, shortening him by a few centimetres. He never complained, bravely displayed his stump. He fought, counted the days until he would be discharged, refused to be put in an old people's home.

His partner begged me, 'Please use you influence to see that they look after your father. I'm sure you have connections.'

Impotent as he was, he remained insufferable and proud. No quiet acceptance of the approach of death for him.

'How do you see your funeral?'

'What are you talking about, Pascal my son? I'm fit as a fiddle, I'll be out of here in no time at all, dammit.'

If he'd told me once, just once, that he'd made mistakes and maltreated my mother, I'd have taken him in my arms, we'd have had a good cry together, I'd have seen him through to his end as gently as possible. But no, he persisted in his mania. There were times when he wanted everyone shot: Marlene Dietrich, the traitor who'd sung for the Yanks, the little pickpockets, the thieving Roma, the people who used stolen cards in cash dispensers. To set an example! 'I'd stick that lot up against the wall,' was his favourite expression. He reminded me of Alcazar, the general in *Tintin* who was regularly defeated by his adversary, General Tapioca, and who, at the least disagreement, would send anyone who spoke out against him to the firing squad.

In hospital my father, freshly shaved, hair trimmed, was dressed in a strange garment halfway between an astronaut's outfit and a disposable nappy. Growing old we find ourselves in a body that doesn't belong to us any more and goes its own way: our organs deteriorate, our sense of shame relaxes, our sphincters as well, it's a continuous symphony in fart major, a return to the infant state without the charm of a child. He wasn't at all embarrassed by it. I would push him round the corridors in a wheelchair and he would sound his little private horn. No sooner had I got to his ward than all I wanted to do was to get away again. I couldn't bring myself to kiss him, I barely brushed his cheeks; I should have taken his hand, pressed it between my palms. I found contact with him repulsive. He was delighted by my visits, they were too much for me. One of life's minor tragedies: the same situations don't have the same quality for those involved in them. Lunch with a former girlfriend is a special event for the man who's been rejected, a mere formality for her. We're out of tune with each other.

He had reached a state where very little was happening in his life: he had nothing to talk about apart from his treatment, the progress of his recovery. His life was restricted to an account of his daily aches and pains. He could fill a good half hour speaking ill of his nearest and dearest, his favourite sport, running my son down in my presence, running me down in my son's presence, after which he'd exhausted his store of slander. He brooded over things in an endless monologue, muttering abuse of the government, doctors, humanity in general. It was a nightmare to imagine that he might live on for another five or ten years, going back and forth between the convalescent home and the clinic, obliging me to bind my life to his. Sometimes it was too much for me and one day, in front of my horrified son, I exploded, 'When is the old bugger going to die, for fuck's sake!'

I was annoyed with myself at that outburst, even though I'd never been more sincere. Who can say whether our children won't be relieved when we die? He gave me a nasty look. Now the boot was on the other foot, he was at the mercy of everyone else. I couldn't see any fear, any plea for pity at all in his look; it was hundred-per-cent-proof rage. And a warning: one day you'll be in my position and you'll pay for it, your son and your daughter will avenge me. Despite myself I admired his pride: old bastard that he was, he still had guts. He was itching to insult me, he was humouring me. Sometimes he lost patience and raised his voice. I would bawl louder and leave, slamming the door. I would come back, conscience-stricken. He was turning me into a torturer. But he kept his fear of death to himself. Hardly had I left the hospital than he would call me, asking if I'd got home safely. A journey on the *métro* or by bus had become an adventure in a foreign land. He wanted to stay in contact at all costs.

He loved crime novels, just as I do. I told him about Sartre admitting he preferred reading whodunits to Wittgenstein. I used to buy new ones for him every week but he didn't like them any more, found them too violent, too vulgar. As far as literature's concerned our tastes differed just as much once we went beyond the classics. I'd given him my copy of *Lady into Fox* by David Garnett, a member of the Bloomsbury Group. Following a hunt in the woods, an English gentleman is amazed to see his wife turn into a vixen with a bright red coat and slip away into the undergrowth. He accepts the metamorphosis and lets her leave every night to join her brother foxes. She comes back in the morning covered in mud, torn and scratched. He had been scandalised by the story, a marvellous metaphor of femininity as wildness. He dumped it in the rubbish bin, from which I went and retrieved it. The idea that my own mother could one day have turned into a cat or a canid and gone off to frolic on the roofs or out in the country drove him mad. I still hadn't lost hope of converting him to my tastes, preferring to share rather than argue with him. My son, a specialist in IT, wanted to introduce him to the Internet. He refused. He detested computers and made his ignorance into a rebellion against modernity.

His favourite game was to go in detail through the great estate he was going to bequeath to us, as if he were Rockefeller or Rothschild in person.

'Three Dutch seascapes, 18th century!'

'Copies, Papa, hardly worth 50 euros each.'

'Your mother's Rolex watch.'

'A fake, Papa, bought in a Delhi market twenty years ago – two euros maximum.'

'A pearl necklace I gave your mother, very expensive.'

'Another fake! I've had it valued.'

'My property in the Luberon?'

'Nothing but stones at the bottom of a ravine. Just about all right for goats but nothing else. Even the solicitor doesn't want to be bothered with it.'

He would boast, go on and on about his possessions, lord it over his sister and his nephews while in fact he was worse than stony broke. Several times I'd told him I'd disclaim his inheritance, since I didn't want to take over his many loans. He'd been offended, as if I were insulting him.

Geriatric medicine comprehends all ailments plus one and that one is beyond remedy. As you pass from ward to ward, you feel like cosseting every patient or suffocating them with a pillow. Some seem so light, their bones hardly weighing more than their skin: carrying them must be like carrying a cloud. You're entering a sterilised hell where the damned, connected up to all sorts of machines, are screaming at their helplessness. The corridors are overrun with amputees, whining, calling for help among the general indifference. This whole herd of pseudo-corpses was falling down around my father, who showed no regret as he watched them succumb. He kept a macabre account. Every time one was carried off to the morgue, he would shout, 'Good riddance!' He alone was still going strong: he was going to outlive the lot of them. He ticked them off one by one, as so many victories. He was going to return home, leaving behind him a trail of corpses. I found his cynicism reassuring, seeing it as a sign of vitality.

Can one ever say enough about the quality of French public services, open to all without distinction of financial situation or nationality? The hospital was staffed by women from the West Indies and all parts of Africa: their youthfulness, their devotion to their patients was a compensation for those trying visits. These women are saints who put all their energy into their work and are paid peanuts. To be honest, it was them I went to see. He wasn't insensible to their charms himself: he had his favourites, notably a beautiful Kabyle woman on whom he lavished interminable history and geography lessons. He was determined to persuade her that France had done everything in Algeria. She listened to him with admirable patience, he talked without stopping, he was the historian and storyteller of the amputation ward. Unfortunately normality was quickly resumed and one day he yelled at an Ivorian, who hadn't brought the bedpan quickly enough, 'You'd do better to climb back up your tree, you lazy monkey!'

After that she refused to go back into his room. He was astonished: 'Aren't those people sensitive, you can't say anything to them.'

I reprimanded him like a badly brought-up child and suggested he apologise. Wasn't he ashamed of calling people names like that – people who came every day to wipe his bottom and change his nappies?

'But you're looking at the question entirely the wrong way round, Pascal. They're the ones who should be happy to be serving me. It's thanks to people like me that they've found work.'

When I went to discuss the incident with the charge nurse, she shrugged her shoulders. 'Oh, these old men, no one listens to them any more. What they say is of such little importance.'

I was even more appalled by this show of indifference than by my father's insulting remark. Another time I arrived to find him exasperated: as he was getting out of the shower an African nurse had asked him, 'Now have we given our little man a good wash, M'sieu Bru'ner?'

I thought it was a delightful expression and adopted it at once. He was never satisfied: the treatment left much to be desired, the food was revolting, the doctors were always vague, the surgeons in a hurry, no one was interested in his case. An infant with a crumpled face, constantly moaning, who was cleaned and changed, he illustrated the law of permanent dissatisfaction in a democracy: whatever is done for any given person, it will never be enough. The more they receive, the more they complain. When I was weary of his verbiage, I would say to him, 'Do you know how much you cost society? Twelve hundred euros a day for your room alone, with board and lodging. And that's not counting the treatment, the operations, the examinations. And you pay nothing at all for all that.'

'Oh come on, I've paid my contributions all my life, I'm not a parasite, like all those Africans, those Roma, those Kurds.'

One day, exasperated by this dying man in top form who was thriving on our exhaustion, I asked him, apropos of nothing, 'Don't you think you should do a Stefan Zweig?'

'What are you on about?'

'You know very well. At the end of his life Stefan Zweig committed suicide, in Brazil, out of despair at the state of the world and the rise of Nazism. Don't you feel tempted to anticipate the call?'

He was horrified. But if he'd accepted my suggestion I would have been the one who was horrified. He'd developed an aversion to Stefan Zweig: he thought his writing, contrary to that of Schnitzler or Werfel, was something for adolescent girls, and he'd put an end to his life in a gesture my father considered cowardly, 'effeminate'. At every visit I would praise the beauty of a voluntary death.

'You're welcome to do it, my dear Pascal, for me it's out

of the question.'

I was annoyed with myself for having gone on about it, but at the time I'd very much enjoyed our exchanges. With a certain smugness I described to him the primitive tribes in which the ancestors go and hide in the forest to die.

To cheer himself up, he would go off on his diatribes again. He had his own Office of Jewish Affairs at home and kept his records scrupulously; he showed touching stamina in his hatred. His opinion of Israel changed every day – one day it was an exemplary state, the next an abominable nation, a country of wops with no traditions – he far preferred Iran, heir to the great Persian civilisation. He didn't like immigrants or violent demonstrators but he drew hope from the fact that in certain suburbs men wearing a *yarmulka* were being hounded. Hitler's posthumous victory in certain sectors of the Arab-Islamic world gladdened his heart. He looked on approvingly as the crowds in Gaza, Cairo or Beirut gave voice to their hatred of the 'Zionists'. True, the slovenly Islamic fundamentalists didn't have the smart marching order of the SS but at least someone was taking up the baton. On the other hand he was sceptical about the French, Hungarian or Greek ultranationalist groups. They were too fat: what distinguishes the Nazis of yesterday from their contemporary avatars is corpulence. Watching a goose-step march past in Paris, Athens or Budapest is to observe the ravages of beer, popcorn, hamburgers, moussaka and goulash on the warriors of the nation. They're all fattened up, clothed in black T-shirts that reveal rather than conceal their spare tyres. They have no class, all they have is bellies. Like a good part of the extreme right, he still preferred the Arabs to the Jews, despite some reservations. He also liked the preacher Tariq Ramadan, 'a good-looking lad who speaks well' – and dared to attack Israel. As for François Hollande, candidate for the presidency at the time, he could only be a Jew, like all the French whose surname is that of a town or a country.

'And Valérie *Trierweiler*,[23] where do you think she comes from with a name like that?' he went on, as if he were called Dupont or Dupuis.

There was one question that obsessed him: had my mother fallen ill to a hereditary disease? Was there a syphilitic germ in her family that had been kept hidden from him, a shameful defect?

'You know, Pascal, in Germany in 1939 they would have gassed your poor mother.' (It was always your 'poor' mother, the attribute attached as to an eternal saint.) 'Epilepsy was considered a degenerative disease. We wouldn't have been able to do anything about it.'

Now his craving for extermination had extended to his own wife: she hadn't deserved to live either. One day he jubilantly waved an article in the *Frankfurter Allgemeine Zeitung* of 21 January 2011 at me: an interview with Stéphane Hessel in which the former member of the Resistance declared:

> Compared with the Israeli occupation of Palestine, the German occupation of France was relatively innocuous, leaving aside certain exceptions such as the imprisonments, internments and executions and the theft of works of art.

'So what do you and your Jewish pals have to say to him, a former *Maquisard*?'

I continued to take him history books in the vain hope they would open his eyes: a monograph on Heydrich by Edouard

23 Journalist and writer (b. 1965); Trierweiler is her married name.

Husson, for example. Without realising it I behaved like an addiction counsellor. I fed him reduced doses of his passion, weaning him off it progressively: Goebbels' *Diaries* on the one side, followed by Christopher R. Browning's study of the *Einsatzgruppen* (military death squads) on the other. The poison and the antidote. He leafed through them with a doubtful look on his face and gave them back to me the next day. Nothing he didn't already know. He hardly discussed these things with me at all any more because I was, as he said to my son, 'Jewified to the core.' But passion is stronger than prudence and our last conversations were peppered with that kind of outburst, especially when he wanted to send the whole of Wall Street to the electric chair after the 2008 crisis, that is to say Madoff, the directors of Lehman Brothers and of Goldman Sachs. He had a proselytising hatred. To put it in a nutshell, we were engaged in two incompatible projects of persuasion. I was always expecting him to say, 'I was wrong,' while he was still hoping I'd admit, 'You were right.' An aggressive zombie, now at death's door, now a loud-mouthed windbag, he had become, like flies stuck to fly-paper, fused with the object of his anger. I found his morbid logorrhoea exhausting. Stupidly, I'd hoped for a redemption, what I got was a confirmation.

The disease was progressive. One day I received an urgent call to go to his flat. His right foot was now gangrenous. He had difficulty walking, I was more or less carrying him. He was trembling. For a moment, overwhelmed with power, I was tempted to let go of him. Make him pay for everything in one go. At that very moment he slipped out of my hands, collapsed to the floor. It was a horrible moment, to see the old man lying on the floor, to see my own father unable to get up, was heart-rending. I felt guilty. I'd thought it and he'd fallen. I was reminded of Ella Fitzgerald, who'd ended her days blind, both of her legs, partly amputated because of diabetes, on a chair. He was amputated the next morning. The cut was slow to heal. He would proudly exhibit his mutilations like war wounds and couldn't understand why we'd turn away in revulsion. One week after the operation he welcomed me one morning with a great rapturous smile. 'D'you know, I've just had a marvellous dream. I was in a town where the flags were out, the children were singing and waving banners in a long procession.'

'Oh, that's very poetic.'

'You think so too? Just imagine, it was in January 1933, the day of Hitler's nomination as chancellor. The people had come out en masse to acclaim him. He was driving round in a beautiful Mercedes convertible. Everything was still possible.'

We spent the whole day talking feet. He knew all there was to know about the blood irrigation of those appendices and orthopaedic techniques. He'd be able to walk again with special shoes supplied by social security and relearn the locomotion function. He had unbelievable get-up-and-go (to coin a phrase). That whole floor of the hospital was full of reduced men like himself in more or less advanced stages of decomposition. In the day room scrawny silhouettes in pyjamas or track suits were watching an American soap opera, *The Young and the Restless,* dubbed into French, mouths open, vacant looks on their faces. Sometimes a delicious aroma of spices would fill the corridor: the nursing auxiliaries and doctors would be making themselves a couscous or a curry in their kitchen and for an hour or two the fragrance would suppress the smell of disinfectant. On Sunday I found him at mass with other patients. He'd never been very devout, he found it a distraction. A priest was promising the dying patients the joys of paradise, an eternity of bliss, the whole bag of tricks. They sang hymns, soon God was going to receive them – much good would it do them. A nun, African or Bengali, kissed all the participants. My father grimaced when she placed a kiss on his cheek: ‘The bullshit these Holy Joes talk!’

When I learnt of his death on 18th August 2012, in a laconic SMS from my son that I got at five in the morning, I was on holiday with the rest of my family and friends on the shore of Lake Powell in the American West, pony-trekking between Arizona and Utah. A ventricular arrhythmia had caused heart failure at lunchtime. He hadn’t suffered. I was both relieved and worried. My first thought was: now the bloody hassle’s going to start. A thin trickle of sadness was submerged in a flood of apprehension at all the procedures that had to be gone through. I wasn’t wrong about that and realised that I was going to get bogged down in an administrative quagmire. I still am. Fortunately my son dealt with the most onerous bits. Bureaucracy grants everyone a kind of imitation eternity that can last for years when you get letters or invitations for someone who’s dead. Even today, when someone rings and calls me by my father’s Christian name, I reply, ‘Sorry, I’m dead, I can’t talk to you any more.’

Still, I was devastated. I’d thought he was invincible. God had waited more than half a century to answer my prayers, His mind must have been elsewhere for a damned long time in the interval. In the meantime a different relationship between my father and myself had become established: the anger had subsided without love taking its place. What I felt for him was a somewhat shamefaced affection mixed with exasperation. I no longer had the strength to hate him. I had forgiven him – out of exhaustion. I listed the good negative reasons not to abhor him completely: after all, he could have killed me in a fit of rage, beaten me up, my mother had made herself a shield to protect me; he could have refused to pay for me to go through university, sent me out to work in a factory at fourteen, he could easily have been much worse. In the final reckoning I had been very lucky considering the disasters I'd avoided. That is the way I exonerated him. Above all it was my son I had to console. He'd developed very close ties with my father and had found him in his bed, his jaw dislocated. I had to comfort my daughter as well, she'd had a fit of hysterics and was sobbing; it took us a long time to calm her down. Her grief, that of a young woman confronted with the horror of mortality for the first time, made me cry, not something new in itself. In Ancient Rome one became *major*, that is adult, on the death of one's father. It had taken me until I was sixty-three to stop being a minor; it's hardly surprising, then, that I spent such a long time stagnating in adolescence.

Our last telephone conversation had been two days previously when I'd rung him from Mesa Verde in Colorado. He had immediately recalled the Amerindian cave-dwelling civilisation that had disappeared in the 14th century as a result of dramatic climate change or a population collapse. He was reading *Pot Luck*, the tenth volume in Zola's *Rougon-Macquart* series, the story of a block of flats in Rue de Choiseul in Paris and the affairs, adulteries and separations connected with it. The title referred to the pot of boiled chicken, the indigestible broth of poor households. We'd had a pretty long chat, as if the distance made our conversation easier. As I hung up, I'd said to my daughter, 'You have to give it to the old man, he's still got all his wits about him and more even.'

When we got home I was introduced to the delectable world of funeral parlours, that combination of compassionate rhetoric and financial mathematics. I loved the obsequiousness, the soft voices, the fixed smiles of the undertakers. The intention of their exaggerated gestures is to distract us from our grief and they sometimes succeed in that. At Hauteville, where he was buried on a lethally cold 1 September in the cemetery with a high-tension wire running over it, the unctuous staff were transformed, after the entombment, into jolly guys who took off their jackets to place the marble slab on the grave with a mechanical crane. I liked their good-humoured approach and for my part I hope my interment will be celebrated with feasts and laughter and not with miserable tears. Looking at the family vault, where my father had several times invited me to rest between him and my mother, while there's also a place left for my son, I said to myself, 'Rather a common grave than that godforsaken hole.'

The philosophy of a funeral involves delicate negotiations: coffin in pine, coffin in oak, in mahogany, handles of wood, brass, copper, interior lined with silk, every article invoiced according to a delicate gradation.

'You poor father had to be given treatment: 700 euros.'

Translated into plain French: part of his face below the eye had fallen in and the thanatopractors had demanded a little repair. He'd had to be patched up quickly.

When I got back from America, I refused to view his body and asked them to seal the coffin. I wanted to retain the cheerful image of the old man who, from the window of his convalescent clinic in the eastern suburbs, had said goodbye to me and my daughter as we were setting off on holiday, certain we'd see him three weeks later. His health was improving, no doubt about that, his voice carried easily to us. That tired face had expressed a hope of reconciliation, the joy at having a family that would carry on his name. His radiant smile, his waving hand also said that every man is more than just himself and bears within him resources of goodness of which he's unaware. For a moment he'd been touched by the light, redeemed.

Since my parents died I keep on coming across them in the street, even abroad, stooped, taking little steps. They return to haunt me in the shape of people I don't know, all the old-age pensioners of France speak to me of them, give me their news. Although born a Protestant, my father had asked for a ceremony in Saint-Etienne-du-Mont on the Montagne Sainte-Geneviève in Paris, the church where he'd got married, where my mother herself had been entitled to a funeral mass. The building is an historic monument and also has literary connections since, among other things, it's there that Eugène de Rastignac attends the funeral mass for Old Goriot, stripped of his last sous by his daughters on his deathbed and 'loving even the ill they did him.' I contacted the parish priest, a robust warrior of the faith such as Catholicism still produces. He deplored the unbelief of the French, their lack of conviction: 'There's something wrong with this country.'

For the service he billed me 500 euros in cash, with no receipt, plus a little tip for the officiating priest, i.e. himself.

'But Father, I thought the Church had made a vow of poverty?'

He scowled but didn't reply. We had a further matter to argue over: the nature of my request. A full mass or a basic service? He'd had enough of these services where no one crossed themselves, no one took communion, no one kneeled. The Church wasn't a supermarket. He wanted fervent devotion or nothing. I told him straight out, 'Father, there'll only be two types of people attending: Jews and communists. Perhaps two or three practising Christians who are able to receive communion. If you don't like it, we'll cancel the whole thing.'

Poor Papa: he who dreamt of world domination by the

Aryan race, the reign of the Blond Beast, was cared for in the hospital by African or Muslim nurses, his granddaughter Anne was Jewish, his last daughter-in-law Rwandan. In addition he had his mass celebrated by a priest who mispronounced his name several times before a sparse gathering (thirteen years ago my mother had had a full house) and got through everything in 40 minutes. As for the book of condolence, there was just one signature – a Korean tourist who had misunderstood and thought it was the church's visitors' book. As we came out, a group of young people was rehearsing a choreographed dance to the music of Elton John, a singer my father loathed because of his way of life. The funeral service was followed by a marriage, doubtless more lucrative. Sometimes God does have a sense of humour.

Epilogue

Exposed

In February 2012 I had an early-morning call from the emergency services of the Ambroise-Paré Hospital in Boulogne. My father had just been admitted in a very confused state. His life wasn't in danger but it was taking a long time for his mind to clear. Arriving there an hour later, I found him in a kind of separate cubicle formed by movable partitions, tied down in his bed. He had bruises everywhere, a puffed-up face, split lips, one cheekbone bleeding. He had fallen, fortunately without breaking anything, and stayed on the ground for a long time, risking congestion of the lungs. He was delirious, rambling, muttering. They'd dressed him in a sort of blue skirt that came down to his knees. I was struck by how white his legs were, with no hair, like a young man. At one point he grew agitated and threw back his tunic. I saw him naked.

I stared, wide-eyed: he'd been circumcised. There was no doubt about it. It was clear. I bent down to make sure it wasn't a hallucination. He was relaxed, entirely exposed. One thing that shocks us about our parents' nudity is that it reduces them to the general condition, emphasises skin blemishes. They are people like all the rest. The taboo doesn't hide what is different but what is similar. I remembered that when I was nine in Lyons I had an operation for a phimosis, a tight foreskin, something common in young boys. My parents had begged the surgeon not to circumcise me in case a war should break out again. The specialist had made no promises and kept none.

Once my father was back in his right mind again, I pestered him with questions. How had he been able to get through the war, settle in Berlin and Vienna, at the heart of the storm, with such a stigma, risking being reported? Or had he had the operation after 1945, when that kind of treatment was still very rare? He denied everything, shocked by my interrogation. He told me to stick to my own business. I got the family together, questioned relations, no one had known. Why had he not even given me an explanation?

I will never know.

There is just one thing I am sure about: my father helped me to think better by thinking against him. I am his defeat, it's the best present he could have given me.

As the horizon shrinks I have one line to follow: not to change anything in my life, to confirm all the choices I've made. I will go without having learnt anything apart from the exorbitant price of existence.

The world is an appeal and a promise: there are remarkable people everywhere, masterpieces to be discovered. There is too much to want, too much to learn and lots of pages to write. As long as you're creating, as long as you're loving, you're still alive.

I hope to remain immortal until my final breath.